THIS USED TO BE
DALLAS

HARRY HALL

Copyright © 2020 by Reedy Press, LLC
All rights reserved.
Reedy Press
PO Box 5131
St. Louis, MO 63139
www.reedypress.com

No part of this publication may be reproduced or transmitted in any form or by any means, electronic or mechanical, including photocopy, recording, or any information storage and retrieval system, without permission in writing from the publisher. Permissions may be sought directly from Reedy Press at the above mailing address or via our website at www.reedypress.com.

Library of Congress Control Number: 2019952735

ISBN: 9781681062617

Front cover: *Texas Hideout Tripod (top); https://texashistory.unt.edu/ark:/67531/metapth599399: accessed August 30, 2019, University of North Texas Libraries, The Portal to Texas History, https://texashistory.unt.edu; crediting Historic Mesquite, Inc. (bottom)*
Back cover: *From* Oh Thank Heaven! The Story of the Southland Corporation, *published by the Southland Corporation; author: Allen Liles (left); Library of Congress (middle); San Diego Air and Space Flikr Archive (right)*

Printed in the United States of America
20 21 22 23 24   5 4 3 2 1

ACKNOWLEDGMENTS

Librarians and researchers: Staff members at the Dallas Public Library, especially Misty Mayberry; Molly Tepera of the Dallas History and Archives Division; John Slate of the Dallas Municipal Archives; and Amy Berry, library coordinator of Highland Park United Methodist Church.

Interviews and insiders: Michael Sarelli, Joe Snowgold, the volunteers at the Dallas Firefighters Museum, Mark Davies of the John F. Kennedy Presidential Library and Museum, Jessica Schneider of the Dallas Jewish Historical Society, James V. Roy, Steve Bonner, Marla Watson, Dr. Robert Vaughn, Bill Marvel, and Mark Stuertz. Writers: Members of the DFW Writers Workshop, specifically Larry Enmon, Daryle McGinnis, Don "Eggs" Eggspuehler, Katie Bernet, and Cliff Morris.

Those who supplied me with invaluable information: Pat Blalock (my mother-in-law), the Dallas Historic Preservation Program, and the Dallas Historical Society.

Could not have done it without you: Charles Breckenridge, whose collection of books about Dallas proved an incredible assistance throughout my research; University of Dallas archival librarian Shelley Gayler-Smith, whose remarkable resources, connections, and tireless efforts contributed mightily to this book; everybody at Reedy Press for their patience; Tui Snider, for recommending me for this project; and my wife Susie, who gave me great ideas and follow-ups for this work and supported me throughout its development and completion.

CONTENTS

Introduction 1

Where Bonnie Parker Made an Honest Living 2
The Mystery and Intrigue of Campisi's Restaurant 4
The Home of Ray Charles 6
When Pegasus Dominated the Skyline 8
Dry Above, Wet Underground 10
When Winfrey Point Served as a POW Camp 12
From "Ho, Ho, Ho!" to "Howdy, Folks!" 14
For Dallas Blacks, the Pythias Temple Had It All 16
Where Dallasites Watched the DJs Work 18
Dallas Bar Association Buys the Belo Mansion 20
It Will Always Be the Texas School Book Depository 22
Crockett School Part of Neighborhood Revitalization 24
When WWI Pilots Trained in Dallas 26
New Technology Replaces Cobb Stadium 28
Musical History Made at 508 Park Avenue 30
Antebellum Mansion Moved to Old City Park 32
Dallas's Top Outdoor Dining Experience? 34
Slave Descendants Delivered from Little Egypt 36
Kidd Springs Park: A Great Place for Families and Feasting 38
Texas's Only Playboy Club 40
The Many Villages of Sam Ventura 42
Streetcars Transform Jefferson Boulevard 44
Multiple Lives of the Davis Building 46
Pedestrian Bridge Gives Underserved Families
    Recreational Opportunity 48
Carnegie Brings Libraries to Dallas 50
Has Tragedy Kept the Texas Theatre Alive? 52

What Is the Future of Dallas's First Motor Hotel?	54
Jump-Starting the West End Marketplace	56
The Home of Dallas's Bandit Queen	58
Beyond Its German Roots	60
Concrete Viaduct Replaces Washed-Out Wooden Bridge	62
A Beer Baron Upends City Hall	64
Exchange Park Advances Dallas Business Atmosphere	66
West Dallas Finally Connects to Mainstream Dallas	68
Spanish Flu Derails Military Training Camp	70
Dallas Welcomes the Fair Park Fire Station	72
Hotel St. Germain Sets the Standard for Excellence	74
Doak Walker Plaza Honors a Legend	76
The Unlikely Revival of the Filter Building	78
Farmers Market District: Symbol of Dallas Growth	80
The Sportatorium: Host of Pro Wrestling and the King of Rock 'n' Roll	82
The One-Time Coffin Company Now Offers Luxury	84
The Southwest's Greatest Playground	86
This Gas Station Housed a Killer	106
Arts Magnet School Earns National Acclaim	108
The Brothers Who Redefined the Retail Industry	110
When Blacks and Whites Lived in Different Worlds	112
The Theater That Wouldn't Stay Down	114
Old Mill Restaurant Maintains Nostalgic Character	116
America's Most Decorated Soldier Owned This Farmhouse	118
A Tragedy That Transformed the World's Health	120
Attention-Getting Billboard	122
Parkland Memorial Hospital Moves Forward	124
Dallas's First Home	126
A Cook-Off That Inspired an International Restaurant Chain	128

Has the Continental Gin Building Gone Bust? 130

From Old Red Courthouse to Museum 132

Tootsies Continues Predecessor's High Standards 134

Musical Venue Expands, But Remains True to Its Roots 136

DART Preserves Monroe Shops 138

The Ladies of Frogtown 140

Woodruff Robbed of Record? 142

Dallas Moves the Trinity River 144

Lucky Lindy's Reputation Nosedives 146

Dallas's Last Vaudeville House 148

Cumberland School Makes Huge Transformation 150

Interurban Rail Creates Progress in Transportation 152

The Colorful Legacy of the Longhorn Ballroom 154

Dying 110-Year-Old School Gets New Life 156

Will Millennials Hang Out at This Former A-List Hotel? 158

The Lakewood Theater Is Spared 160

When Dallas Put Trains Underground 162

A Major Golf Tournament Got Its Start Here 164

It Really Was a Bomb Factory, Sort of 166

Plans for Cedars Development Go Up in Smoke 168

The First International Hotel Chain Started in Dallas 170

The French-Influenced Wilson Building 172

Dallas World Aquarium: More Than Fish 174

Don't Mess with My Tex-Mex 176

Not the Cowboys' "Field of Dreams" 178

The Little Oak Cliff Store That Grew to Worldwide Prominence 180

Women's Center Honors One of Dallas's Great Ones 182

Inn of the Dove Was a Godsend for Blacks 184

Babe Didrikson: "The Dallas Wonder" 186

vii

The Statler Still Thrives 188
Gables Republic Tower: More Than "The Rocket" 190
A History of Dining Innovation and Convenience on Lower Greenville 192
The Bookstore That Encourages Conversation 194
Eagle Ford School: The Last Remnant of Mexican American
    Pioneers 196
Did Lone Star Lofts Serve as a SEAL Training Ground? 198

Sources 200
Index 209

INTRODUCTION

I thought I knew Dallas.

After all, we lived just seven miles away when President Kennedy was assassinated, and three miles from the theater where his killer, Lee Harvey Oswald, was captured.

When I accepted this assignment from Reedy Press, my first thought was Dallas's famous waterfall billboard. I was probably just a preschooler when my mother introduced me to this mesmerizing sight—all that water flowing over those rocks, easily seen from IH-35 near downtown where each day thousands of commuters could marvel at its wonder. The magnificent waterfall billboard could stand alone. The series of advertisements, originally for beer and cigarettes, gets in the way.

Other places I researched were familiar to me as well. In my younger days, the roughly 10-mile jogging trail around White Rock Lake was a great place for serious marathon training; the Texas State Fair which, except for one year, my now college-age son and I have visited since he was three; downtown's fascinating Triangle Point Building, whose glassed-in second floor opened the world of big-time radio to passersby who could watch DJs spin records from the home of Dallas's number one radio station, KLIF: the "Mighty 1190."

Yet all these places held secrets.

My joke to friends was, "You can't have too much Kennedy assassination and Bonnie and Clyde." Sure, it was flippant, maybe even disrespectful, but those were defining moments in the city's history.

"But how," I repeatedly asked myself, "can you cover a city's 100-years'-plus growth in 90 one-half column-length subjects?"

Had Reedy Press done my hometown a disservice?

I spoke with city veterans, plunged through books, made notes on hundreds of cards, looking for 90 clues, 90 stories, 90 places that would help me relay to you what brought Dallas from nothing on a river to an international city.

I think I got it right. If you really know this city, you'll relive some memories. If you think you know it, then buckle up, because you are in for a few surprises. If you are new here, you will discover a new adventure on every page. Whether you are new to Dallas or a "Big D" veteran, you will see the city in a whole new light.

I know I do.

Where Bonnie Parker Made an Honest Living

The semi-circle driveway that rounds the corner at 3308 Swiss at Hall St. doesn't look like much except for the front entrance—which is a plyboard on hinges—and the windows around it, the entire single-story building is painted black. The inside has been gutted amid rumors of a revitalization. The structure has survived several close calls. Nearby Baylor University Medical Center and Dallas Theological Seminary both expanded without harming it. Since its creation in 1915, the building has been home to a variety of places: a TV/stereo store, a tire shop, Evans Tree and Stump Work, and AA offices.

But its most significant identity was probably that of Hartgraves Café, opened by Mrs. Alcie (aka "Elsie" or "Alice") Hartgraves in 1923, months after the death of her husband, Ben.

From 1928 to 1929, one of Hartgraves's waitresses was a teenager named Bonnie Parker.

This was before she met Clyde Barrow, before the couple made national headlines traveling from state to state robbing banks and killing those who got in their way, before she wrote the poem that foretold their premature deaths, "The Story of Bonnie and Clyde."

Apparently, the waitress was much different than the criminal she became. In 1972, Rose Myers, who worked at Yates's Laundry, which faced the rear of Hartgraves, knew Parker and said she was "a very nice person" and "easy to get along with." Bonnie didn't meet Clyde until after she left the restaurant, which closed in 1931.

Not long after Bonnie left Hartgraves, a mirror and glass company located a half-mile west at 2614 Swiss Ave. hired Clyde Barrow.

The buildng is now under renovation to become a new eatery. (Photo by Harry Hall.)

While the semicircular structure has suffered years of neglect, a group of investors is looking to turn it into a restaurant, and it might happen. Presumably for additional parking, the group leveled the adjacent Floyd's Jewelry Store.

Maybe the new restaurant will work and keep alive another small part of the legend of Bonnie and Clyde.

THIS USED TO BE: Hartgraves Café
NOW IT'S: Abandoned (proposed restaurant)
LOCATION: 3308 Swiss Ave.

The Mystery and Intrigue of Campisi's Restaurant

The Sicilian-born Campisi family had run a grocery store in Dallas since 1904. In 1946, after a cousin suggested they try selling a New York favorite called pizza pie, family patriarch Carlo "Papa" Campisi opened Dallas's first pizzeria. In 1950, they moved from their original location at 4548 McKinney (at Knox) to 5610 E. Mockingbird Lane, just east of the Southern Methodist University campus, where they bought the Egyptian Lounge, a 1940s modernist nightclub with limited parking. After paying for the indoor renovation, the Campisis had only enough money to change one word on the sign. They called their new venture "The Egyptian Restaurant" (the Campisi's name was added later).

The popular restaurant still offers a variety of Italian favorites, such as lasagna, pizza, and spaghetti, but also hamburgers and cheeseburgers. Campisi's has also generated controversy. For years, the restaurant operated on a cash-only basis. Rumors spread of illegal bets being made at the restaurant's bar. Joe Campisi, who had at least one mafia boss friend, was identified in Drug Enforcement Agency files as having ties to organized crime, and the Federal Bureau of Investigation used to photograph anyone who entered the restaurant. Conspiracy theorists linked them to the Kennedy assassination, since Campisi's regular, Jack Ruby, supposedly ate there on November 21, 1963, just two days before he shot Lee Harvey Oswald. Just nine days later, the then-jailed Ruby requested and received a 10-minute meeting with Joe Campisi.

In an article published by the *Los Angeles Times* on February 14, 1999, David Campisi said of all the rumors: "The public always ate it up. We've never played off it like we should."

In 1991, Major League Baseball umpire Steve Palermo, while trying to rescue a woman from an assault outside Campisi's, was shot and paralyzed.

For years the restaurant was rumored to have ties to the underworld, but that might have been part of the cost of doing business. In addition to regulars such as Jack Ruby, Dallas Cowboys' coach Tom Landry also ate there. (Photo by Harry Hall.)

THIS USED TO BE: The Egyptian Lounge nightclub
NOW IT'S: Campisi's Egyptian Restaurant
LOCATION: 5610 E. Mockingbird Ln.

The Home of Ray Charles

In some ways, the two-bedroom, one-bathroom bungalow at 2642 Eugene St. at Matilda, just southwest of Malcolm X Blvd., represented the upcoming racial revolution that would change Dallas. According to Dallas historian Darwin Payne, in 1951, a racially motivated bombing happened just four houses down, the result of the resentment whites in the neighborhood felt toward the growing Black population.

No one knew it at the time, but that unassuming house would have historical musical significance.

Soul singer Ray Charles lived there from 1955 to 1958, when he and his pregnant girlfriend, Della Beatrice Howard, left the Green Acres Courts Motel.

Before moving to Dallas, Charles had already scored hits with "Confession Blues" in 1949 and his first hit with Atlantic Records in 1953, "Mess Around." He moved to Dallas for travel convenience, and he might also have felt at home in a city that was once home to blues legends Huddie William Ledbetter ("Lead Belly") and "Blind Lemon" Jefferson. Ultimately, Charles just wanted to live here. He wrote in his autobiography *Brother Ray: Ray Charles' Own Story*, "I knew the town, and I dug it."

Charles practiced and wrote music on the electric piano he kept in his living room with saxophonist David "Fathead" Newman, with whom Charles developed a close friendship. He also played in venues such as Woodman's Hall and the Empire Room. Those sessions and performances helped him score some minor hits such as "I Got A Woman" and "Hallelujah I Love Her So."

The house has no visible sign of significance. In early 2017, it sold for $10,000; it was recently appraised for $83,000.

Frank Sinatra called Ray Charles "the only true genius in show business."

This house's location gave Ray Charles easy access to Woodman's Hall, the Empire Room, and the Arandas Club, where he would jump in and play jam sessions with locals. (Photo by Harry Hall.)

THIS USED TO BE: Ray Charles's home
NOW IT'S: An abandoned bungalow
LOCATION: 2642 Eugene St.

When Pegasus Dominated the Skyline

Just in front of the Omni Hotel, at the corner of Akard and Main Street, is Pegasus Plaza, a 16,000-square-foot shaded area that includes seating and fountains. It's used for many city events, from concerts to Christmas celebrations. The biggest attraction is the red neon-lighted horse Pegasus, which measures 42 feet wide and 40 feet tall and sits atop a makeshift oil derrick. Pegasus has been a big part of Dallas since 1934, but its history started in the late 19th century. In 1869, Vacuum Oil, which produced petroleum-based lubricants for horse-drawn carriages and steam engines, adopted a red gargoyle as its trademark. In 1911, a company subsidiary first trademarked a Pegasus logo. As demand for gasoline and automobiles grew, Vacuum Oil expanded, eventually morphing into Mobil. The winged horse known as Pegasus was placed on top of the Magnolia Petroleum, making the 29-story structure the tallest west of the Mississippi. The glowing rotating red figure was mounted on a 22-foot-high oil derrick, and for decades beginning in 1934, it welcomed visitors entering Dallas or those returning from a road trip. Pilots claimed they could see it while flying over Hillsboro, 60 miles to the south; others said it could be seen from Waco, 40 miles south of that.

In 1959, Magnolia Oil became Mobil, and the new company adopted Pegasus as its official symbol.

As the years wore on, Pegasus was dwarfed by taller buildings, and its bright red color faded.

After more than six decades of guiding and greeting visitors and home folks returning from a trip, a deteriorating Pegasus was retired in 1999 and replaced with a more understated one, smaller and anchored. The newer symbol relit the Dallas skyline on January 1, 2000.

In Greek mythology, Pegasus carried lightning bolts for Zeus.

The restoration process for the original Pegasus was kept secret and given the code "Miss Peggy." Conservator Michael van Enter was hired for the project, using custom-built submersion tanks and developing a compound for which to soak the pieces. They cleaned the parts with sponges. Van Enter said, "Basically, 70 years of dirt and corrosion came off." (Photo by Madison Berndt Creative Commons 2.0.)

THIS USED TO BE: The highly visible Pegasus atop the Magnolia Building

NOW IT'S: A smaller and understated Pegasus atop the Magnolia Hotel

TIP: Red horse images can be seen throughout Dallas

Dry Above, Wet Underground

When Lincoln Properties bought the land at 600 N. Akard St. in the early 1980s, they sought to build one of the city's most high-class restaurants that would accommodate hungry visitors to the nearby arts district.

And that's what they did. Dakota's Steakhouse exudes elegance with its wood-paneled walls, New Orleans-style gas lamps, a courtyard, firepit, wine room, and a menu (updated about twice a year) that includes steak aged for at least 28 days. Since 1984, Dakota's has served as one of Dallas's most stylish and romantic restaurants. Its biggest drawback might be that Dakota's is impossible to see from the street. In fact, the only ground-level proof that it exists is a sign and valet parking kiosk. Capitalizing on its unique existence, it uses the clever tagline, "Underground Steakhouse, Above and Beyond Expectations."

Dakota's Steakhouse was built 18 feet underground.

Here's why. The First Baptist Church of Dallas, one of the largest and most influential churches in the country, owned the property. Then under the pastoral guidance of W. A. Criswell, it boasted a congregation of more than 20,000.

The restaurant's website says, "The site was once occupied by the First Baptist Church of Dallas, who put a legally binding clause in the deed that prohibits any future owner from selling alcohol on former church grounds."

But legally, "on the ground" doesn't mean "under the ground."

Lincoln offered to build the restaurant underground, and the proposal passed muster with both the city and Dr. Criswell, who might have thought Lincoln would never do it, so the sale went through. Since then, Dakota's has thrived. Patrons get to the restaurant via the elevator, where alcohol is not sold.

The word *Dakota* comes from the Sioux language and means "forever smiling."

The elevator is canopied glass that overlooks Dakota's 1,800-square-foot subterranean courtyard, where guests are introduced to a five-tiered granite water wall, multi-tiered landscaping, lava rock firepit, and black granite bar. (Photo by Harry Hall.)

THIS USED TO BE: Property of First Baptist Church of Dallas

NOW IT'S: Dakota's Steakhouse

LOCATION: 600 N. Akard St.

When Winfrey Point Served as a POW Camp

Winfrey Point overlooks scenic White Rock Lake and might be the park's most visible landmark. It has the look and feel of an old building: multi-paneled windows, a concrete porch that leads to a wooden door, a creaky wooden floor that echoes with any step, no air-conditioning, and little or no insulation.

Although more than 80 years old, Winfrey Point remains a popular spot for many levels of Dallas society. It hosts weddings, family reunions, and business meetings. Its most frequent use is as a pre- and post-race hangout for the road racers of the Dallas Running Club and other amateur athletic events. Its attraction is easy to see. Looking west from its high perch on the lake's southeast bank, you get a striking view of the lake and the Dallas skyline.

Winfrey Point was a project of the Civilian Conservation Corps, one of President Franklin Roosevelt's first programs under the New Deal. For the next several years, 3,000 CCC workers enhanced the park, which included building the lake's retaining wall, picnic areas, the Big Thicket Cabin, and Winfrey Point. Later, the barracks that housed the young people served as an induction center and boot camp before soldiers headed off to World War II.

From December 1944 to August 1945, Winfrey Point housed 300 German prisoners of war, all of whom were members of General Erwin Rommel's Afrika Korps. The prisoners used barbed wire to build an eight-foot-high fence around the compound. Buses transported many prisoners to Fair Park's Centennial Building, where they repaired military

After the war, Southern Methodist University used the barracks as overflow student housing for post-GI students. Today, the buildings are gone, replaced by baseball fields.

The POW camp stood where these baseball fields are today. The Winfrey Point house, which was built by the German POWs, sits at the top of the hill on the left. (Photos by Dallas Municipal Archives.)

equipment and uniforms. Several times, suspicious neighbors reported seeing prisoners on the loose, but no prisoner escape was ever recorded. During their free time, prisoners painted or stenciled pictures on barrack walls and tended to their gardens.

THIS USED TO BE: A German POW camp

NOW IT'S: Home for parties and receptions, and a popular hangout for runners

LOCATION: 951 Winfrey Point Way

From "Ho, Ho, Ho!" to "Howdy, Folks!"

"Howdy, folks! Welcome to the great State Fair of Texas!" Even non-fairgoers will recognize that memorable line that is heard about 60 times a day during the fall at the fair's annual three-week-plus run. The speaker, of course, is Big Tex, who qualifies at 55 feet tall, with 12-foot-long boots and a 95-gallon hat, making him the perfect mascot for the nation's largest fair.

The mascot's genesis goes back to the small town of Kerens, Texas, located about 100 miles south of Dallas. Howard Brister, the Kerens Chamber of Commerce manager, was looking for a gimmick to encourage local Christmas shopping, instead of driving 15 miles west to Corsicana. He came up with a giant Santa Claus.

The giant Santa smiled and waved at locals, and it worked, but the novelty eventually wore off. Dallas's R. L. Thornton bought Santa for $750. Thornton hoped to create a massive public relations blitz in Fair Park to help boost Christmas sales, but then someone suggested the giant Santa be turned into a Texas image and become part of the 1952 State Fair. Thus, Big Tex was born and became an instant hit.

Upgrades and remodeling occurred over the years. Tex's nose was shortened, his right arm was tucked near his shoulder, the papier-mâché head was replaced with fiberglass, and his clothes were periodically changed.

In 2002, in celebration of his 50th birthday, some gray hair and wrinkles were added, and he received an honorary membership to the AARP.

During the last weekend of the fair in 2012, Tex's right boot caught fire, and in just a few minutes, the symbol of the Texas State Fair was consumed in flames. The next year saw a new Big Tex, which continues to carry on the 67-year Big Tex and Texas State Fair tradition.

The Texas State Fair attracts about two million visitors each year.

The face of the Texas State Fair has undergone several changes since his inception as Santa Claus in 1949, but his welcoming voice and powerful presence have been a constant. He's been modified through age, clothing changes, and even a fire in 2012 that couldn't keep him down. (Big Tex 2010: Creative Commons 2.0; Big Tex 2016: Creative Commons 2.0.)

THIS USED TO BE: Santa Claus

NOW IT'S: Big Tex

LOCATION: 1300 Robert B. Cullum Blvd.

For Dallas Blacks, the Pythias Temple Had It All

From 1916 to 1939, the Beaux Arts-style Grand Lodge of the Colored Knights of Pythias Temple was almost a one-stop facility for middle-class Blacks in Dallas. Designed by Black architect William Sidney Pittman, the structure at 2551 Elm St. in Deep Ellum featured neoclassical red brick and tall, arched windows. It was Dallas's first building built by Blacks, for Blacks, and with funding by Blacks.

Need a haircut? Pythias Temple had a barber. Want something from a drugstore? Got one. Feeling poorly? Or suffering from a toothache? Doctor's and dentist's offices were on the third floor. Looking to enjoy an evening of dancing? Ballroom, fourth floor.

Services ranged from necessary to entertaining and educational, and they were wildly popular with the underserved community. Major attractions included the Fisk Jubilee Singers, Black activist speaker Marcus Garvey, and Pittman's father-in-law, George Washington Carver.

Citing financial difficulties, the Knights of Pythias was forced to sell in 1946; it was sold again in 1956. After purchasing the building in 1959, the Union Bankers Insurance Company turned it into office space.

In 1989, the city declared Pythias Temple a Dallas landmark. In the 1990s, the Union Bankers abandoned the site.

Several attempts have been made to renovate and revitalize the crumbling building, the most ambitious and controversial being to build a hotel as part of the renovation. If completed, the current proposal is to name it after the architect of the original structure more than 100 years ago: "The Pittman."

The Knights of Pythias was the first fraternal order chartered by an act of Congress.

In addition to lectures and groups such as the Fisk Jubilee Singers, other notable acts to play in the fourth-floor ballroom included blues legends "Blind Lemon" Jefferson and Sam "Lightnin'" Hopkins. (Creative Commons 3.0. Photo by Joe Mabel taken February 3, 2013.)

THIS USED TO BE: The center for social and entertainment activity for early-twentieth-century Blacks in Dallas

NOW IT'S: A 194-room hotel called The Pittman, named after its architect, William Sidney Pittman (scheduled to open in 2020)

LOCATION: 2551 Elm St.

Where Dallasites Watched the DJs Work

Built in 1930, the Triangle Point Building at 2120 Commerce St. was a gas station associated with the Magnolia Oil Company. The station's home was called the "Triangle Building," which described its shape and location at the intersection of Commerce, Wood, and North Central Expressway. It featured two stories with a drive-through on the first floor that included three bays for customers to gas up.

The curiously shaped building earned its greatest fame from 1964 to 1980, when it became home to Dallas's most popular radio station—KLIF, the "Mighty 1190." The one-time gas bays were remodeled as garages for the radio station's news vans. The upper floor did more than serve as office space and the traditional radio broadcast booth. Dallas drivers and passersby could look up through the glass-walled second story and see a KLIF DJ talking into the station's microphone and spinning records, maybe connecting with its listeners as no radio station had ever done.

The marketing idea was just another in a long list of broadcast innovations for Gordon McLendon. The Paris, Texas, native nicknamed "the Old Scotchman" owned many radio stations and founded the Liberty Radio Network and, with his father, KLIF. A case could be made that McLendon invented the modern radio format. He created traffic reports, the first all-news station, and the radio jingle.

While inviting listeners to see a broadcast was a brilliant marketing gimmick, it also helped that some of the KLIF DJs were major talents. Included were Dallas radio legend Ron Chapman, Jim O'Brien (father of Peri Gilpin of the TV show *Frasier*) and Rod Roddy, later the announcer for many national game shows, most notably *The Price Is Right*.

Today, the Triangle Point Building is the home of Maharger Development.

Popular KLIF DJ Mike Selden in the KLIF studio on Commerce St. in Dallas.

KLIF's first broadcast was on June 26, 1922, as KGKO in Wichita Falls, Texas.

THIS USED TO BE: Home of KLIF radio—The "Mighty 1190"
NOW IT'S: Maharger Development
LOCATION: 2120 Commerce St.

Dallas Bar Association Buys the Belo Mansion

In the mid-1970s, the Dallas Bar Association needed a new home. The organization had outgrown several meeting areas over the preceding 20 years, and they were ready for a permanent place that would accommodate their growth. They targeted the Belo Mansion, which was still owned by the family of *Dallas Morning News* co-founder A. H. Belo. The architect of the 70-year-old neoclassical structure was Herbert Greene, who also designed the family's mansion in Belo's native city of Salem, North Carolina.

The mansion was built on Ross Avenue, the city's first paved road and "upscale" neighborhood. (It's now part of the Dallas Arts District.) In the early days, the family used it as a showcase for cultural and social events. By 1973, longtime lessee Loudermilk-Sparkman Funeral Home had moved out, and three years later, the Bar Association raised the money to buy it. Republic Bank funded the home's extensive remodeling needs, which took more than a year.

According to Bob Thomas of the Dallas Bar Association, A. H. Belo's granddaughter, 77-year old Helen Belo Morrison, negotiated the agreement with the funeral home in 1926, attended the Belo grand reopening in 1979, and said, "Oh my gosh. You've restored my home, my birthplace, just as I remember it as a little girl."

Since the purchase, the Dallas Bar has grown from about 3,500 members to 11,000. Dallas attorneys "hang out" at the mansion, which is one of the finest lawyer headquarters in the country. Many of the one-time Belo family rooms are available for social or business events. The 20,000-square-foot Pavilion at the Belo Mansion can accommodate up to 350 people in four meeting rooms.

In 1934, as Loudermilk-Sparkman Funeral Home, thousands came to the viewing and funeral of gangster Clyde Barrow.

It's believed that construction on the mansion started around 1900, the year A. H. Belo Jr. married Helen Ponder. The couple lived in the mansion with his parents. Sadly, Belo Sr. died the next year at 69. (Photo by Andreas Praefcke, Creative Commons Attribution 3.0 Unported, https://creativecommons.org/licenses/by/3.0/deed.en.)

THIS USED TO BE: Belo family home
NOW IT'S: Dallas Bar Association headquarters
LOCATION: 2115 Ross Ave.

It Will Always Be the Texas School Book Depository

The address is 411 Elm St., at the northeast corner of N. Houston St. It's called the Dallas County Administration Building, but its Romanesque Revival style has been around since its predecessor, a five-story building for the Southern Rock Island Plow Company, was struck by lightning and burned to the ground in 1901. For the last half-century, the now seven-story structure is undoubtedly the most familiar, photographed, and attention-grabbing sight in the Dallas skyline. Every year, tourists from all over the world come to the area, point, take pictures, and speculate.

From 1942 to 1961, it was leased to Chicago-based grocery wholesaler John Sexton and Company and nicknamed the Sexton Building. Sexton moved out, and an extensive refurbishing project took place that included installing air-conditioning. It was then sold to the privately owned Texas School Book Depository.

While it's now called the County Administrative Building, like Parkland Hospital and the Texas Theatre, it will always be associated with the President Kennedy assassination. (Photo by L. Dakota, courtesy of North https://creativecommons.org/licenses/by-sa/4.0/deed.en.)

In 2002, a gallery opened on the seventh floor. Exhibits there have included the works of Andy Warhol. The Sixth Floor Museum at Dealey Plaza is open 10:00 a.m. to 6:00 p.m. every day except Monday, when it is open from noon to 6:00 p.m.

President Kennedy's unpopularity in Dallas made many think the trip to Texas unwise. Passing through a mass of adoring humanity, the First Lady of Texas, Mrs. Nellie Connally, said, "Mr. President, you can't say Dallas doesn't love you." The president responded, "That is very obvious." Those were his last words. (Photo by George Reid; photo courtesy of Sixth Floor Museum, Dealey Plaza.)

On Thursday, November 22, 1963, the Texas School Book Depository became the center of the world when, at 12:30 p.m., Lee Harvey Oswald took aim out of the southeast corner of the sixth-floor window and fired three shots into the car that carried President John F. Kennedy from Houston St. left (west) on Elm, killing him.

After several years of floundering, the building's lower five floors were renovated. In 1981, it was designated for use as offices for the Dallas County Administration Building. The Sixth Floor Museum, dedicated to the assassination, opened on Presidents' Day (February 20, 1989).

THIS USED TO BE: The Texas School Book Depository
NOW IT'S: Dallas County Administration Building
LOCATION: 411 Elm St.

Crockett School Part of Neighborhood Revitalization

The nearly five-minute 2011 YouTube video chronicles the deterioration of the David Crockett School. Walking with a handheld video camera and Sarah McLachlan's "I Will Remember You" softly playing, the operator circles the building, revealing rusted doors and drain spouts, peeling paint, and ancient window-unit air conditioners. Possible remnants of homeless people, piles of clothes, and trash had accumulated on the porches and other school entries. Near the video's conclusion, the phrase "Demolition by Neglect" appears on the screen.

Built in 1903, the two-story Italian Renaissance-style brick building was then one of the city's oldest remaining schools. By the 1960s, it was in disrepair, but it would house students for another 20 years. The school was a microcosm of this East Dallas neighborhood, one of Dallas's oldest, with a high concentration of run-down Victorian-era homes.

David Crockett School was last used regularly in 1989, when it served as an administration building. Like the neighborhood, it didn't appear to have much of a future. Then came an extensive renovation. The city put money into two nearby parks, and residents started Porchfest, an annual event that showcases community artists and musicians to raise money for beautification. Now run by Indio Management, the David Crockett School is called the Principal Residences. It's been revamped, upgraded, and modified, and it now has 52 apartments made from classrooms, the basement, cafeteria, and auditorium. The stand-alone gymnasium is now home to six maple-floor apartments. Larger classrooms were also divided into multiple apartments. It has wide hallways and 18-foot-high ceilings, and the school's water fountains, lockers, and light fixtures are part of the layout. The extensive renovations have helped to maintain the neighborhood's original character.

Like many recent renovations, the David Crockett School barely escaped demolition. The building's deterioration made upgrading a challenge. Developer Allen Brown says, "It's great a building like this gets a second life. East Dallas, before it becomes another Uptown, needs things like this to anchor it." (Photo by Harry Hall.)

This neighborhood was settled by Jefferson Peak, a real estate developer who used streetcar lines to promote his developments.

THIS USED TO BE: David Crockett School
NOW IT'S: Principal Residences
LOCATION: 401 N. Carroll Ave.

When WWI Pilots Trained in Dallas

When the United States entered World War I in 1917, the army built a series of pilot training camps throughout the nation. One site was a 700-acre plot just south of Bachman Lake. The new facility included wooden buildings for officers and maintenance and tents for enlisted men. After an initial eight-week training session, prospective pilots were selected for advanced flying instruction. They named the facility Love Field, after 2LT Moss Lee Love. 2LT Love had trained in the Philippines and in April 1913 was ordered to aviation duty at Texas City, Texas, with the 1st Aero Squadron. On September 4, 1913, he was over San Diego's North Island practicing for his military aviator test in a Wright Model C Pusher biplane. According to witnesses, his plane suddenly dropped, and they saw a puff of smoke before the plane plunged into the ground, instantly killing the 32-year-old pilot.

2LT Love became just the 10th aviation officer killed in a plane crash.

For the next several years, Love Field served mostly as a stopping point for planes headed to other destinations. However, in 1923, the military closed it and sold everything as army surplus. The War Department leased the land to local farmers and ranchers.

Dallas purchased Love Field and turned it into a civilian airport. By 1939, it oversaw 21 daily flights. It grew until 1974, when DFW International Airport opened between the two major cities. Enplanements dropped from 6.8 million in 1973 (eighth busiest in America) to just 467,212 in 1975.

However, throughout the 1970s, deregulation and the appearance of no-frills, short-trip Southwest Airlines brought life back to the airport. Other airlines moved in, increasing Love Field's value to North Texas.

In 2017, Love Field's centennial, the airport handled a record 15.7 million passengers.

Above: 1918 US GOV-PD Air Service. (Photo by US Army via San Diego Air and Space Flikr Archive.) Left: Love Field today. (https://creativecommons.org/licenses/by-sa/3.0/deed.en Author Danazar.)

For more than 100 years, Dallas Love Field has served Texas and the country, from training the nation's first military pilots for WWI to taking passengers on commercial flights. (Photo: 1918 Dallas Love Field panoramic photographs, courtesy of Library of Congress.)

THIS USED TO BE: Military training airfield
NOW IT'S: Love Field Airport
LOCATION: 8008 Heb Kelleher Way

New Technology Replaces Cobb Stadium

The Infomart represents what could be called "New Dallas," an ideal example of power and influence of a 21st-century economy based on technology instead of traditional oil and land.

This iron and glass building with a steel frame curtain has more than 1.5 million square feet of office space and seven floors; it was modeled after Britain's Crystal Palace, which was created for the 1851 "Great Exhibition," the genesis of the World's Fair. It stands in a conspicuous part of Dallas at 1950 N. Stemmons, near two other high-profile Dallas landmarks: Market Hall and Kim Dawson Studios (now KD College).

The Infomart replaced PC Cobb Stadium (originally called Dal-Hi), a 1939 WPA project that for decades served as home to many high school athletic contests. By 1981, it had passed 40 years of age and looked old and expendable. Its 22,000 seats were adequate, but concrete bleachers made sitting though any athletic contest an ordeal. It couldn't compete with other more modern and welcoming-looking arenas with better lighting, modern tracks, and comfortable seating. Its virtually all-concrete design made demolition surprisingly difficult.

The Infomart became the world's first information processing marketing center. It serves as a data center and technology office to more than 100 technology and telecommunications companies, including Cologix, Flexential, and Equinix, the latter of which in 2018 paid $800 million in cash to buy the building and changed its name to Equinix Infomart. Equinix then accounted for 40% of the building's office space leasing.

As the Infomart becomes a bigger and more important part of the technological landscape, its future looks enduring and significant.

In 1969, Cobb Stadium played host to the North American Soccer League's Dallas Tornado.

With downtown Dallas visible in the background, members of the University of North Carolina football team prepare at Dal-Hi Stadium for the January 2, 1950, Cotton Bowl matchup with Rice University. The Owls would prevail, 27-13. (North Carolina Collection, University of North Carolina Library Chapel Hill, photographer Hugh Morton; courtesy of Pixabay.)

The Equinix Infomart represents 21st-century technology. (Courtesy of Creative Commons.)

THIS USED TO BE: Dal-Hi/PC Cobb Stadium

NOW IT'S: The Equinix Infomart

LOCATION: 1950 N. Stemmons Frwy.

Musical History Made at 508 Park Avenue

In June 1937, Mississippi-born blues singer-songwriter Robert Johnson came to Dallas for a recording session at 508 Park Avenue. Producer Don Law set up a makeshift studio on the building's third floor. On June 19 and 20, Johnson recorded 13 songs of the 29 that he recorded during his short life, such as "Hellhound on My Trail" and "Traveling Riverside Blues."

Until then, the address and 23,000-square-foot art deco Zigzag Moderne style building was just part of Dallas's Film Row, but in two historic days, the significance of 508 Park Avenue skyrocketed.

Those two days transformed the building and, most importantly, music. Then called the "Brunswick Record Building," the site would over the next several decades see 843 recording sessions from a variety of artists, including Bob Wills and the Texas Playboys, the Light Crust Doughboys, and Lolo Cavazos.

Michael Taft, director of the American Folklife Center at the Library of Congress, observed that "the significance of any building is what we put into it. A building is just bricks and mortar. But 508 Park Avenue is one of two buildings that has a connection with and is part of the story of two of the most important recording sessions in American history. I think the significance is in the event that took place there, every bit as much as the site at Gettysburg is as important as the battle that took place there."

Today, 508 Park Avenue is part of Encore Park, a project of the Stewpot, a community outreach program that, among other benevolences, feeds 1,000 meals per day, seven days a week.

**At 508 Park Avenue in 2004, Eric Clapton recorded segments for the record and documentary film titled *Sessions for Robert J.*

Before the renovation, the building was boarded up for years, and its future seemed bleak. "People would come and touch the building on a sacred pilgrimage," said Carol Adams, an Encore Park committee member. "All around the world, there was this fear that this building would come down." (Photo by Becky Houtman, photographer, https://creativecommons.org/licenses/by/2.0/.)

THIS USED TO BE: Warner Bros. Building

NOW IT'S: Part of the community outreach program, the Stewpot

LOCATION: 508 Park Ave.

Antebellum Mansion Moved to Old City Park

In 1966, after more than 100 years sitting on the same spot on Bonnie View Road and Millermore Street in South Dallas, the Millermore Mansion—Dallas's only one remaining from the antebellum era—seemed destined for the bulldozer. Since the 1850s, a member of the Miller family had lived in the home and now, with the death of the last family member, the house sat in near collapse. It appeared that the white, two-story Greek Revival home had reached an unfortunate end.

William Brown Miller built the Millermore in 1857. Miller was a cotton magnate, Confederate soldier, and Dallas pioneer. After the war ended in 1865, he not only released his slaves, but gave them some of his land. Reportedly, at least one slave family descendent still owns some of that property.

In the 11th hour, the Dallas Heritage Society saved the Millermore by raising $30,000 to pay for its renovation. The mansion was carefully disassembled, and the boards were numbered and sent for reconstruction to join other structures that would also be reassembled in Old City Park—aka Dallas Heritage Village. There, it would become the showcase of a recreated neighborhood that includes about 30 other time-period structures that create an environment for a visit to the past for its 50,000 annual visitors. Admission fees range from $10 for adults to $6 for children, with special rates for groups. The village is open 10 a.m. to 4 p.m., Tuesday through Saturday, and from noon to 4 p.m. on Sunday. It is closed on Mondays and during the months of January and August.

The Millermore is supposedly haunted.

Dallas Heritage Village at Old City Park, where the Millermore is now located, is a great spot for the mansion. The park was established in 1876, just 19 years after the Millermore's construction. (Photo by Gail Frederick, photographer, courtesy of https://creativecommons.org/licenses/by/2.0/.)

THIS USED TO BE: Millermore Mansion in South Dallas

NOW IT'S: Millermore Museum, part of Dallas Heritage Village History and Culture

LOCATION: 1515 South Harwood St., Dallas Heritage Village at Old City Park

Dallas's Top Outdoor Dining Experience?

Saint Ann Restaurant and Bar has done a remarkable job adapting to its surroundings. When erected as a school for Hispanics in 1927, Saint Ann's School was part of what was then called "Little Mexico," where Uptown is today. In 1946, it was enlarged for Dallas's first Hispanic high school for girls, which prepared students for the business world. It closed in 1965.

While progress killed Little Mexico, St. Ann thrived. Physically, it's the same two-story, red brick structure, not far from Klyde Warren Park, the Perot Museum, and the American Airlines Center.

While food and drink are always attractions for an eatery, Saint Ann features a fine wine list and entrees that include salmon, pizza, Angus burgers, and sides such as truffle fries and herb-roasted mushrooms. But Saint Ann might be most famous for its outdoor dining. *D Magazine* voted it "Best Patio in Dallas," and OpenTable.com called it "Best Outdoor Dining." According to www.visitdallas.com, Saint Ann "features the largest garden patio in Dallas."

The garden patio is large, with plenty of trees to provide shade during the warmer times—a big part of Dallas weather. It has benches and tables surrounded by towering glass buildings and great views of Uptown. That and a mature, relaxed crowd contribute to a serene atmosphere, whether enjoying a meal or drinks with friends. And the restaurant hasn't forgotten its Hispanic or educational background. One patio focal point is the Our Lady of Guadalupe mural, and drink categories include Jock, the Nerd, Prom Queen, Pop Quiz, and the Overachiever.

The restaurant's second floor is the Ann and Gabriel Barbier-Mueller Samurai Museum, which is free to visit.

CultureMap Dallas says that Saint Ann Restaurant and Bar is "quite possibly the prettiest outdoor space of any restaurant in Dallas. The garden patio is sophisticated yet unpretentious."

THIS USED TO BE: Saint Ann's School
NOW IT'S: Saint Ann Restaurant and Bar
LOCATION: 2501 Harwood St.

Slave Descendants Delivered from Little Egypt

Northlake Center is well-suited for its upscale northeast Dallas clientele. Retail outlets include Tuesday Morning and Northlake Health Food. The center is located on Northwest Highway between Audelia and Ferndale, not far from White Rock Lake, the city's most popular recreation park. But the influence of this shopping center goes far beyond generating commerce for the neighborhood. Its creation transformed the lives of families who had been neglected for generations.

In 1865, just after emancipation, newly freed Dallas slaves needed a place to live. So, the city gave them a 35-acre plot across the street from where Northlake Shopping Center stands today. The residents called their new home "Little Egypt" because the freed slaves believed, like in the Bible story, they had been delivered from bondage. But nearly a century later, Little Egypt looked woefully out of place. The neighborhood had only dirt roads, and the homes lacked electricity, running water, and indoor plumbing.

When the shopping center was built in 1961, rezoning took place, making Little Egypt, then home to about 200 families, desirable by commercial investors. For a year, negotiations were made between the residents, all members of Little Egypt Baptist Church, and even out-of-state heirs. Each resident received between $6,500 and $60,000. The investors paid for all moving expenses.

On Monday night, May 14, 1962, the final service was held in the church, with many praying that forecasted rain would hold off. It did.

The next morning, 37 trucks arrived and spent the day moving the residents. Hours later, Little Egypt, which for 97 years had been home to hundreds of Blacks, former slaves, and their descendants, was effectively no more.

Most residents were glad to leave and begin their new lives in new houses with modern facilities. Some settled in Elm Thicket and Rockwall County. Many accompanied the church's move to Oak Cliff.

Today, the former Little Egypt consists of upscale homes and all the modern conveniences, such as the corner of Thurgood and Shoreview, in what is now Lake Highlands. The catalyst for the neighborhood upgrade was the development of Northlake Shopping Center, which supplanted the residents after buying them out. (Photo by Bill Zeeble of KERA News.)

The real estate deal was made more difficult because some of the homes were built on the wrong plots.

THIS USED TO BE: Little Egypt

NOW IT'S: Northlake Shopping Center and an upscale neighborhood

LOCATION: Lake Highlands NW Highway between Audelia and Ferndale

Kidd Springs Park: A Great Place for Families and Feasting

Almost hidden in the North Oak Cliff neighborhood is family-friendly, largely shaded Kidd Springs Park. Recreation attractions include a recreation center, playground area, softball field, and walking path that circles the park's small lake. Japanese and butterfly gardens add a touch of serenity. It's changed quite a bit over the years.

In 1874, Confederate soldier, auctioneer, and farmer Colonel James Kidd bought 200 acres that included the 31-acre modern park. In 1887, Kidd's son sold the land to Edward Turner, who in 1895 turned it into a private recreation area, known as Kidd Springs Fishing and Boating Club. Later, it was opened to the public, and a fee was charged for use of its large pool, giant water slide, a mill wheel device, and various diving platforms and boards. In 1947, the city bought the facility for $125,000.

Throughout the year, Kidd Springs hosts other family-friendly events, such as the Dallas Festival of the Arts, which displays local arts and crafts and is presented by the Atlanta Foundation for Public Spaces. But the biggest attraction is probably November's Blues, Bandits and BBQ. For two days, grillers from throughout Dallas invade the park, showing off their culinary skills and filling the air with the aroma of a variety of personal creations for preparing pork, tacos, briskets, ribs, and sausage. In 2018, 35 outdoor chefs competed for the coveted People's Choice

In the 1920s, Kidd Springs was home to annual picnics for Confederate veterans. According to a news account, during the 1923 picnic, they discussed lobbying to increase Confederate Army pensions from $8 per month.

In the fall, the Blues, Bandits and BBQ festival brings out creative BBQ masters with no shortage of volunteers to sample the tasty delights. (Photos courtesy of Autumn Keith.)

Awards, chosen by some 2,000 samplers—event visitors who pay $25 for the privilege to sample the tasty morsels. If the food isn't enough, the event also features live blues bands playing throughout the weekend.

THIS USED TO BE: Kidd Springs Fishing and Boating Club

NOW IT'S: Kidd Springs Park

LOCATION: 700 W. Canty

Texas's Only Playboy Club

The 15-story, modern high-rise at the corner of Central Expressway and Mockingbird looks like the perfect spot for the SMU East Campus. A large banner announces it, and a neon galloping mustang (the school mascot) illuminates its west side, facing the main campus. The second floor is part of the school's nerve center, and it hits you with the sterile environment of academic offices. The brown-ribbed carpet absorbs most of the sound that seems out of place, anyway. Barren white walls, no plants, a series of brown doors, labeled with bland paper-shuffling job titles: Accounts Payable, Purchasing, Human Resources—all necessary and unglamorous departments necessary for any business.

But from 1978 to 1982, this floor was home to one of the hottest nightspots in Dallas and was Texas's only Playboy Club.

Dallas resident Lenny Licht accepted a bet that he couldn't bring a Playboy Club to Dallas. While attending school in Boston, he met Christie Hefner (daughter of Hugh) and convinced her and her associates that they should bring one of the then-popular clubs to Dallas. Attractions included young women dressed in either blue or black form-fitting "bunny" outfits, complete with cotton tail and four-inch-high spiked heels. They served drinks but otherwise had limited interaction with customers. The entertainment quality was high and included some of the era's top singers, such as Mel Tormé and Lainie Kazan, and comedians George Gobel and "Professor" Irwin Corey.

The Dallas club opened with much fanfare. Entry required a key, and 50,000 were made. Rumors were that some nights the wait for entry could stretch as much as two hours. But the novelty quickly wore off, as other clubs, not hindered by limited space availability and redesign, diminished the club's glamour, and it closed in 1982.

The third floor was the headquarters for the Dallas Cowboys. Many players, such as Tony Dorsett and Ed "Too Tall" Jones, often hung out there.

The second floor of what is now the nerve center for SMU East Campus was once Dallas's hottest club that played host to top singing and comedy acts. (Photo by Harry Hall.)

Today, the 2nd floor is little more than office space. (Photo by Harry Hall.)

THIS USED TO BE: The Playboy Club (Second floor)
NOW IT'S: SMU East Campus
LOCATION: 6116 Central Expressway

The Many Villages of Sam Ventura

The trio of eclectic restaurants that stand at the corner of 3211 Oak Lawn caters to clientele who use valet parking for their luxury vehicles. Snooze, Sushi Axiom, and Green Papaya represent an upgrade from the building's earlier ownership, but since the early 1930s, the corner of Oak Lawn and Hall St. has been a focal point for Dallas dining.

Originally, the restaurant at that corner was owned by Sam Ventura and his son, Sam Jr. No matter the name—Italian Village, Oak Lawn Village, Village Club, Club Village—until the late 1970s, the Venturas always promoted some feature or enticement to keep people coming. In the years preceding World War II, he installed air-conditioning. For a while, he operated so that liquor could be sold—then an illegal act in a public facility. In 1939, as part of his ninth expansion, he announced a series of rooms, including a marionette show starring puppets made in the likeness of the owners. During World War II, Ventura temporarily dropped "Italian" from the restaurant's name, and it became simply The Village. After yet another renovation in 1961 and renaming as "Club Village," his bar fronted a glass cage that contained live monkeys and two flamingoes named Lancelot and Guinevere.

A remodeling after a 1971 fire resulted in three restaurants at the one address. In 1974, eight years after Sam Sr. retired, Sam Jr. underwent a religious conversion and, over his father's objections, rejected alcohol sales and set up King's Village, which became Dallas's first Christian dinner theater. His nonalcoholic offerings included "Promised Land," a Christian "libation" of milk and honey. Sales plummeted, and of the three eateries, only the Italian Village survived.

The last vestige of the Italian Village closed in the late 1970s.

In 1961, scenes from the popular television show *Route 66* were filmed in Club Village. The episode, titled "A Long Piece of Mischief," starred Denver Pyle and Slim Pickens.

It's unlikely that Sam Ventura could have imagined serving sushi or breakfast at one of his restaurants, but he could identify with keeping up with locals' changing dining habits. (Photo by Harry Hall.)

Sam Ventura's restaurant/club ventures went through many changes and upgrades—a total of nine by 1939—only five years after buying it as a drive-in restaurant from Speck Harper for $250. Sam had to borrow the money. (From Paula Bosse, July 1, 2018, Flashback Dallas.)

THIS USED TO BE: Many "Village" named restaurants

NOW IT'S: A series of cafes and eateries

LOCATION: 3211 Oak Lawn

Streetcars Transform Jefferson Boulevard

The area around Jefferson Blvd. in Oak Cliff largely consists of high-rise apartments and retail outlets. Original structures such as the city hall, fire station, and movie theater are gone. Many early Oak Cliff establishments were torn down during the mid-1950s to make way for Interstate 35. The only long-standing buildings protected from demolition by city ordinance are Sunset High School, Oak Cliff Methodist Church, and Pachanga Wholesale Bridal & Quinceañera, which back in 1912 was the Mallory Drug Store. Mallory, like many area businesses, owed its success to mass transportation.

Shortly after Thomas Marsalis and John Armstrong bought 2,000 acres for what helped jumpstart Oak Cliff in 1887, Marsalis developed a transit line to Dallas, the first reliable transportation across the Trinity River. Jefferson Blvd. became a major stop for electric street cars and the Interurban. Originally planned for residential development, Jefferson Blvd. became the lifeblood of Oak Cliff. The businessmen suddenly saw it as an opportunity to build along the electric transit line, which ran down W. Jefferson and north on N. Tyler St., where Mallory sat on the southwest corner. That stop helped the drugstore take root and become a major part of Oak Cliff life. In those days, the drugstore was also a lunch counter, a place to drop off mail, and even a spot to get a car registered.

In the subsequent decades, however, cars overtook streetcars in popularity, and the neighborhood lost much of its economic and social advantages. Later, Mallory became one of many Clarence Saunders grocery stores and, eventually, B&B Bicycles. In 1998, it was named a Dallas landmark.

In August 2016, a new Oak Cliff streetcar began servicing the Bishop Arts District. Many locals hope it will one day extend to Jefferson, just like in the old days.

Early in the 20th century, the trolley track can be seen running right in front of the Mallory Drug Store, which helped make Oak Cliff a substantial retail area. The transit not only traversed Oak Cliff, but linked with the interurban transit, taking people to Ft. Worth. (From the George W. Cook collection, Southern Methodist University.)

Radio station KLIF took its call letters in honor of Oak Cliff.

THIS USED TO BE: Mallory Drug Store

NOW IT'S: Pachanga Wholesale Bridal & Quinceañera

LOCATION: 900 W. Jefferson Blvd.

Multiple Lives of the Davis Building

The newly renovated Drakestone promotes itself as "a place where 1920s elegance meets contemporary downtown loft living." All have exposed brick and concrete accents, and "every loft has incredible views," whether looking over downtown or across the Trinity River into Oak Cliff. Amenities include windows with solar shades, restaurants, retail outlets, direct access to the Dallas tunnel system, cleaners, and a spa.

The Drakestone has nearly 100 years as part of the Dallas skyline. It has struggled through the years, but it's now one of Dallas's most recognized structures, and it is listed on the US National Register of Historic Places.

In 1926, as the Republic Bank Building, the classic revival building was then the second tallest in the city and home to many companies, including the Texas Baseball League and Coca-Cola Bottling. It also housed four mayors and was the birthplace for Texas Instruments. When the bank moved out in 1954, its cupola went dark, and the Republic Bank Building was renamed for Wirt Davis, longtime Republic Bank chairman.

In the 1970s, with an occupancy rate of 30%, the building fell into decades of floundering. Numerous attempts at revitalization failed; for seven years, it sat for sale and eventually fell into foreclosure. It sold in 1993, and a new renovation plan was proposed, but that failed, too. Finally, in 1997, Hamilton Properties purchased the building and turned the desperate situation into 183 lofts.

The remarkable renovation was completed in 2002, with the relighting of the long-dark cupola. In 2011, with Color Kinetics, the owners upgraded the exterior lighting to a more energy-efficient LED system.

The building was used as part of the set in the movie *Touch and Die*, with Martin Sheen.

The Davis Building is one of many historic buildings on Main Street near Akard and Ervay. Its neighbors include the original Neiman Marcus store, the Adolphus Hotel, and the Magnolia Building. (Photo by Steven Leggett, courtesy of https://creativecommons.org/licenses/by/2.0/deed.en.)

THIS USED TO BE: Republic Bank Building

NOW IT'S: The Drakestone 183 lofts, stores, office space, and commercial outlets

LOCATION: 1309 Main St.

Pedestrian Bridge Gives Underserved Families Recreational Opportunity

By itself, the Ronald Kirk Bridge doesn't seem nearly as important as its two neighboring bridges. The multi-span girder bridge made of concrete and steel reaches more than six football fields across the Trinity River into Dallas. But it's far less spectacular than the adjacent cable-stayed $117 million Margaret Hunt Hill Bridge. The Kirk Bridge is only about one-third the length of the more substantial Jefferson St. Viaduct to the south, which serves as a vital vehicular artery from Dallas to Oak Cliff. And the city's original vision for the Kirk Bridge was far different.

In disrepair and already under reconstruction in 2010 when, as part of the Trinity River Project, the city determined that the MHH Bridge sufficiently served West Dallas vehicular traffic, so the Kirk Bridge was converted from the Lamar-McKinney Viaduct (aka the Continental Avenue Bridge) to pedestrians only. The results were spectacular.

Thousands turned out for the June 15, 2014 (Father's Day) Ronald Kirk Bridge ribbon-cutting ceremony. Mariachi bands, bocce ball, food trucks, and other family activities filled the day. The pedestrian bridge gave the frequently forgotten West Dallas residents convenient foot access to Klyde Warren Park, a five-acre, family-oriented area that is just a 1.5-mile walk east on Continental above the recessed eight-lane Woodall Rogers Freeway.

Since its opening, the Kirk Bridge remains an attractive playground for families who want to stroll, ride rented electric scooters, climb on the Kompan Blox playground, or just relax on a sunny weekend afternoon.

Pedestrians can also enjoy many walking trails in proximity to the bridge, the Trinity River Basin, and nearby levees.

Originally called the Lamar-McKinney Viaduct, the Continental Avenue Bridge was designed as a thoroughfare across the Trinity River from downtown to West Dallas. The bridge was completed 27 years after the Great Flood of 1908 that devastated Dallas. (Photos by Patrick Feller.)

THIS USED TO BE: The Continental Avenue Bridge

NOW IT'S: The Ronald Kirk Bridge (pedestrians only)

LOCATION: Connects Continental Blvd. to West Dallas

Carnegie Brings Libraries to Dallas

In 2017, the *Dallas Morning News*, shrinking in both circulation and staff and recognizing a need for more technological innovations, moved from its 68-year-old home on Young Street. Its new residence, one-third the size of the original, was 1954 Commerce Street—the site of the Old Dallas Public Library. A great example of mid–20th-century architecture, it featured four aboveground floors (with provisions for two more) and two underground floors. The building was designed by George Dahl in 1953, and it replaced Dallas's original library.

In the spring of 1899, Mrs. Henry Extall, president of Dallas's City Federation of Women's Clubs, determined to help raise money for a Dallas library. She made a good start, collecting $11,000 from Dallas citizens, including from the *Dallas Morning News* owner A. H. Belo.

For the rest, she wrote to US Steel founder-turned-philanthropist Andrew Carnegie, who would eventually oversee the creation of 3,000 libraries across the nation. Carnegie had recently donated $50,000 to Fort Worth for a library. Extall convinced him that Dallas was also worthy. She received the donation, contingent on Dallas providing the site and spending $4,000 per year for maintenance.

On October 22, 1901, the two-story, French Renaissance-style Carnegie Library opened at the southwest corner of Harwood and Commerce Streets with almost 10,000 books. In 1914, a second Carnegie Library opened at 500 E. Jefferson (at Marsalis), making Dallas the only city in the country with two Carnegie libraries.

By the 1950s, both Dallas Carnegie Libraries were deteriorating. The main library was demolished in 1954. The Oak Cliff Library was razed in 1967 and is now Turner Plaza.

Oak Cliff artist Frank Reaugh donated a painting to the main library's second floor. That donation became the catalyst for the Dallas Museum of Art.

Andrew Carnegie believed that a library served the public but was supported with public funding, which is why his agreements included communities putting up maintenance funds. (George W. Cook Dallas Image Collection, 1909; photographer unknown.)

THIS USED TO BE: Main Carnegie Library and North Oak Cliff Library

NOW IT'S: Dallas Morning News (main) and Turner Plaza (branch)

LOCATION: 1954 Commerce St. (main) and 500 E. Jefferson Blvd. (branch)

Has Tragedy Kept the Texas Theatre Alive?

The art deco-style Texas Theatre, with the distinctive vertically arranged yellow, red, and blue "T-E-X-A-S" neon sign, each letter highlighted with a star, has made history since it opened on San Jacinto Day, April 21, 1931. The theater, then the third largest in Dallas, was once partially owned by Howard Hughes and the first in town built for talkies and air-conditioning. It's suffered through the years with increased entertainment competition, financial problems, multiple closings, and a fire. But it remains in its original location at 231 W. Jefferson, a bustling area that has seen big change in the neighborhood, with mostly Hispanic-themed businesses up and down the street.

The Texas Theatre drew international attention for its connection with the assassination of President Kennedy on November 22, 1963.

After shooting the president, Lee Harvey Oswald fled from downtown to Oak Cliff, shot an off-duty officer, and sought refuge in the Texas Theatre, where he entered without paying. Hearing the tragedy playing out on the radio, noting Oswald's description, and troubled by his suspicious behavior, a theater employee called the police—15 arrived to arrest him.

Attempting to distance itself from the tragedy, the theater was reconfigured inside and out. A Spanish-stucco redesign covered the star-and-cloud-painted ceilings. In early 1965, it got a new facade and new screen, and the auditorium was reupholstered. To discourage sneaks, the stairwell was turned 180 degrees, and the ticket office was moved inside.

In 2003, the Texas Theatre was added to the National Register of Historic Places, a move that might have saved it from demolition. Next, after several years of abandonment, the newly formed Aviation Cinemas reopened the theater in 2010. It's now home to a variety of movies, concerts, and events, most notably the Oak Cliff Film Festival.

For years, controversy surged through Dallas as many attempted to distance themselves from the tragedy through hiding, denial, and even destroying the Texas Theatre. While it closed and was left for dead several times, today it has been revitalized and is a valuable, respected, and recognized structure for its significance in local and US history. (Vintage photo: Osbornb, courtesy of Creative Commons 2.0 Generic. Modern photo: Texas Theater in Dallas by Michael Dorosh, Wikimedia Commons.)

In 1991, the then-owner Texas Theatrical Society gave approval to Oliver Stone to remodel the facade for the film *JFK*.

THIS USED TO BE: Texas Theatre, the area's first air-conditioned movie theater

NOW IT'S: Texas Theatre, home to several events, most notably the Oak Cliff Film Festival

LOCATION: 231 W. Jefferson Blvd.

What Is the Future of Dallas's First Motor Hotel?

The Belmont Hotel looks far older than it should. Its green sign is faded, and its Art Moderne design with emphasis on horizontal lines, rounded corners, and stucco facades probably should have gone through a greater revitalization. The hotel looks out of place at the busy intersection of Sylvan and Fort Worth Avenues. Its most recent renovation in 2005 gave it a few years of life, but it hasn't kept up with its more modern surroundings, a sad state for one of Dallas's most historically significant lodges.

The cost to build the Belmont Motor Hotel in 1946 was a staggering $400,000 at the time ($5,242,000 in 2019). Construction on Dallas's first motor lodge, which was perched on a West Dallas hilltop, included moving 8,000 cubic yards of dirt to give its visitors a clear view of the growing Dallas skyline. It even used the slogan "the motel with the Sky-View of Dallas." Other advancements included fireproof masonry and air-conditioning. The hotel became a popular spot for everyone from out-of-towners to those just wanting to hang out.

The Belmont lost its uniqueness during the 1950s as other hotels installed air-conditioning. The multipurpose Sylvan Thirty Apartments moved in and blocked much of the Belmont's skyline view. In addition, the radio station 91.7 FM ended its popular KXT "Barefoot at the Belmont Concert" series.

A recent move to protect the hotel from demolition by making it a Dallas landmark was reportedly made "to keep [others] from tearing it down." That move is currently still in discussion. The owner has a vision for the property. He wants to do another renovation on the long-standing structure, but for now, the Belmont Hotel's fate remains in limbo.

Once an innovative, creative place for out-of-towners or locals to enjoy a weekend, deterioration, lack of direction, and competition from newer hotels with more innovative amenities have meant an uncertain future for the Belmont Hotel. (Photo by Nan Palmero, courtesy of Creative Commons 2.0 Generic.)

Belmont Hotel designer Charles Dilbeck was a self-taught architect who earned a reputation for both hotel and residential designs.

THIS USED TO BE: Belmont Motor Hotel
NOW IT'S: Belmont Hotel
LOCATION: 901 Ft. Worth Ave.

Jump-Starting the West End Marketplace

The Spaghetti Warehouse is within easy walking distance of just about everything in the West End, including the DART bus line, which stops right in front of the two-story, red-brick, one-time pillow factory. When the Spaghetti Warehouse opened in 1972, the area was still known as the warehouse district, and it consisted of aging, unsightly buildings that no longer held significance for the city. With its success, the West End expanded with many other restaurants. Museums and shops have opened, such as Dick's Last Resort and Ellen's, and patrons can enjoy a stroll through the area or the post-dining experience of a horse-drawn carriage ride. The transformation has made the West End Marketplace a popular night spot in Dallas, with more than seven million visitors annually.

The restaurant's entrees are made with the same ingredients as when they were prepared by original chief chef and executive vice president Victor Petta Jr., who followed generations-old family recipes that resulted in great from-scratch spaghettis and meatball dishes. Additional menu items include Tuscan ribs and calamari. But the tasty and reasonably priced food is only part of the dining experience. The restaurant also offers a fabulous family-dining atmosphere enhanced by a décor that includes an old confessional and the headboard and footboard from one of Stephen F. Austin's beds, which were transformed into a booth that holds up to eight people.

What stands out most is an actual East Dallas streetcar, used in the late 1800s for transporting folks to what is now the West End. The Spaghetti Warehouse closed on October 20, 2019.

Paranormal activity has been associated with the Spaghetti Warehouse.

Each Spaghetti Warehouse restaurant had a trolley inside. Many of the restaurants were originally warehouses that dated back to the late 1800s to early 1900s, and trolleys frequently served these areas. (Photo by Harry Hall.)

• •

THIS USED TO BE: A pillow factory

NOW IT'S: The Spaghetti Warehouse (recently closed)

LOCATION: 1815 North Market St.

• •

The Home of Dallas's Bandit Queen

Belle Starr Drive looks more like a glorified alley. Only about 75 yards long, it dead-ends into a field. On one side of this southeast Dallas street sits two single-family frame houses with small, fenced yards and a Daily Mart on the corner. Opposite these structures and facing Scyene Road is a Family Dollar and a laundromat. However, this nondescript neighborhood boasts a hidden colorful history. In the 1870s, the area was a farm owned by John and Elizabeth Shirley, whose daughter Myra was the street's namesake, Belle Starr.

The road isn't the only thing named after one of Dallas's most colorful characters. She might be the only person who had a church and bar named after her. Starr was the subject of several books and at least two movies. A statue of her stands in Ponca City, Oklahoma.

Not bad for someone nicknamed "Queen of the Bandits."

Separating fact from fiction in regard to Belle Starr might require a time machine. Born Myra Belle Shirley in 1848 in Missouri, her family moved to Dallas during Reconstruction. She was undoubtedly a crack shot who hung around unsavory characters, such as the outlaw Cole Younger and maybe even Jesse James. And those outlaws probably did use the Shirley home as a hideout. However, she likely wasn't as adventurous as portrayed in the day's dime-store novels, which had her robbing banks and murdering people.

The last remnant of that era to disappear was a two-story barn near Scyene and St. Augustine that once served as a school. It was there that Belle Starr married stagecoach robber Jim Reed and made a living running a livery stable in East Dallas that dealt in stolen horses.

On February 3, 1889, Belle Starr was shot in the back in Oklahoma. No one was ever charged with the killing. She was 41 years old.

Belle Starr's life might have been more legend than fact, but in the 1870s she was probably Dallas's most famous and notorious resident. She reportedly associated with, and maybe gave comfort to, some famous outlaws. She married Jim Reed, who was associated with Cole Younger and Jesse James. (Photo courtesy of Wikipedia.)

Little is left of the remnants of the 1870s Shirley homestead, but at one time the area included the family barn, which once served as a school. (Photo by Harry Hall.)

THIS USED TO BE: Home of Belle Starr

NOW IT'S: Belle Starr Dr.

LOCATION: Southeast Dallas at the corner of 352 Scyene Rd. and Belle Starr Dr.

Beyond Its German Roots

The history page of the Sons of Hermann Hall's website reads, "Proud to be the oldest free-standing wood structure in Dallas. And also, the oldest bar!"

Built in 1911, Sons of Hermann Hall's century-old wooden design looks out of place amid the modern structures that surround it on Elm Street. The Hall has a five-bays-wide symmetrical front facade with several one-over-one double-hung windows. The original wood siding has been replaced with asbestos shingles. It has a low mansard roof with composition shingles and high parapets and eaves supported by ornate brackets. Sons of Hermann was founded in New York in 1840 in response to anti-German sentiment due to the millions of German immigrants who were flooding into the country.

Originally, only German was spoken at their meetings, adding to their goal of maintaining their national heritage in America. In 1917, bowling lanes were open, and competition between lodges was common until the 1960s. Remnants are still visible in the Old Bowling Alley Room. Beginning in the 1930s, the need for the meetings diminished, and music became a bigger part of the lodge's makeup, with a men's chorus called the Frohsinn Singing Society and a dancing group known as the Schuhplattens.

Since the 1980s, Sons of Hermann Hall has seen some impressive musical performers. The one-time meeting facility now serves as a dance hall and music venue. Acts that played there include Arlo Guthrie, Asleep at the Wheel, and The Chicks. In 2002, eventual *American Idol* winner Kelly Clarkson passed her first audition at Sons of Hermann Hall.

In one episode of the hit TV show *Dallas*, Sue Ellen is committed to Meadowlark Sanitarium, which was really the transformed meeting room on the first floor of Sons of Hermann Hall.

Since its transformation into a live music venue in the 1980s, Sons of Hermann Hall has found a vital niche in the Dallas entertainment community. The May 1990 issue of *D Magazine* called it "one of the top 10 neighborhood bars left in Dallas." (Photo by d double u, licensed under CC BY-SA 2.0, https://creativecommons.org/licenses/by-sa/2.0/.)

THIS USED TO BE: A meeting hall/lodge
NOW IT'S: A music venue/event center
LOCATION: 3414 Elm St. (at Exposition)

Concrete Viaduct Replaces Washed-Out Wooden Bridge

On April 20, 1908, torrential rains all over the southwest spilled into the Trinity River. The *Dallas Morning News* reported that the Trinity had crested at 29 feet, making it the third-worst flood in Dallas history.

The paper could not have been more wrong.

Later that year on May 24 and 25, the river still stood at 28 feet when 15 more inches drenched the city. For three days, the city faced downed electrical and telephone lines, polluted water, and grounded trains. Looters stole surviving livestock, and people and animals were stranded on roofs, in trees, and on debris that flowed down the swollen river. A rancid odor engulfed the city.

Estimates of damage ranged up to $5 million ($136 million in 2019), and 5,000 people became homeless. More distressing, "the long wooden bridge"—since 1890, a crucial lifeline that crossed the Trinity and connected Dallas's Cadiz Street to Jefferson Street in Oak Cliff washed out—separated the two cities.

In response to the catastrophe, citizens passed a $650,000 bond package ($16.9 million in 2019) to build what was then the Oak Cliff Viaduct—now known as the Houston Street Viaduct. The grand opening in 1912 drew a crowd of 58,000.

The Houston Street Viaduct became one of Dallas's most city-defining structures. The open spandrel concrete barrel arch structure stretches more than a mile. It's supported by 51 reinforced concrete arches, a 44-foot-wide road with four and a half feet of sidewalk on each side. The foundation was created when piles were driven into the ground and concrete was poured in around them. For more than 100 years, it has been the main artery for people traveling across the Trinity River to and from Dallas and Oak Cliff; it's had few modifications and has never flooded.

Katy engine moving freight cars from flood in Katy Yards.—Dallas, May 25, '08.

Other than a concrete handrail added in the 1930s and the addition of stairs at the Reunion Arena parking areas, the Houston Street Viaduct has not undergone any visible modifications. (US Library of Congress, Prints and Photographs Division, Built In America Collection, https://www.loc.gov/pictures/collection/hh/, photo by Joseph E. B. Elliott.)

One newspaper wrote, "Oak Cliff is cut off from the rest of the world and hundreds of families driven from their homes and left idle." The only mode of transportation was a paddleboat steamer, which took people down the Trinity River that was full of houses, cows, hogs, sheep, and other objects. (DeGoyler Library, SMU, May 25, 1908.)

For several days, boats were enlisted to rescue people stranded on houses and floating debris. The police chief said those efforts saved 500 to 1,000 lives. One boat's crew witnessed an entire house collapse and disappear after rescuing 16 family members from the rooftop.

THIS USED TO BE: The Long Wooden Bridge
NOW IT'S: The Houston Street Viaduct
LOCATION: Connects central Dallas business district with Oak Cliff

A Beer Baron Upends City Hall

The impressive Adolphus Hotel stands 22 stories tall at the northwest corner of Commerce and Akard Streets, the heart of downtown. The building attracts attention without even trying. Loosely modeled after Chicago's Blackstone Hotel, it was nicknamed "the gingerbread palace." One writer called it "a wondrous combination of French Renaissance and beer baron architecture." The hotel has 422 rooms, 25,000 square feet of meeting space, a 5,500-square-foot grand ballroom, and two junior ballrooms. One of its more elegant features is the weekend's "high tea," featuring "House Made Savory Tea" and a light menu that includes sandwiches and scones. Amenities include a spa and pool with a rooftop bar.

St. Louis native and self-made beer magnate Adolphus Busch made Texas the first out-of-state destination for delivery of his beer in refrigerator cars, and Texans gave his cold brew a warm reception. In 1910, he sought to expand his empire, wanting to build a luxury hotel in Dallas.

He told officials that he wanted the corner of Commerce and Akard or nothing. Busch apparently didn't care that the spot he selected for his new venture was home to Dallas City Hall. On June 22, 1910, the city sold the land and building to Busch.

The hotel opened on October 5, 1912, at a cost of nearly $1.9 million ($50 million in 2018). Busch described it as "the first grand hotel in Dallas." Of the original 875 rooms (many were lost during an extensive renovation), 275 were air-conditioned. Overnight rates started at $2. The Adolphus Hotel helped to boost the careers of famous actors, including comedians Bob Hope and Jack Benny. Queen Elizabeth II has even stayed there.

Since the 1930s, the ghost of a jilted bride reportedly has been seen wandering the 19th floor.

The old city hall is on the left; it was replaced by the Adolphus (right). Stories of several mysterious deaths at the Adolphus have led to rumors that it's haunted. At least two people fell down elevator shafts. (Photo by Joe Mabel, https://creativecommons.org/licenses/by-sa/3.0/deed.en, photo of 1908 card courtesy of DeGolyer Library SMU.)

THIS USED TO BE: Dallas City Hall

NOW IT'S: Hotel Adolphus, Part of Marriott's exclusive Autograph Collection Hotels

LOCATION: 1321 Commerce St.

Exchange Park Advances Dallas Business Atmosphere

In 1956, 120 acres near Harry Hines and Mockingbird Lane were transformed into the 14-story Exchange Park building, the first step in a proposed and expansive "city within a city," "city of tomorrow," and "a self-contained business community—America's first completely integrated and weather-controlled commercial development."

The second phase, the 10-story Braniff building, was completed three years later with bright blue spandrels, a rear facade with a different shading system, and a top floor with a landscaped terrace that gave Braniff Airline executives views of Love Field. A smaller structure, called the Frito-Lay building, was added later.

The grand plan was to include office buildings, shops, services, two department stores, a hotel, and residential towers. The vision never came to full fruition, but what was built was well ahead of its time. Exchange Park included an underground tunnel for the loading and unloading of trucks without obstructing ground traffic. Connecting the two towers were 40-foot-wide "weather-conditioned streets" that were the home to fully enclosed shops, services, and restaurants. It was the precursor to modern shopping malls.

One of the most notable tenants was the La Tunisia Restaurant, a perfect setting for an Arabian night's atmosphere for romance and intrigue, including a menu of Arabian dishes or American fare. The back of the menu read, "Veiled waitresses dressed as harem girls to serve cocktails." Another notable attraction was the Mickey Mantle's $500,000 32-lane Bowling Center, for which 10,000 turned out for the opening in February 1959.

La Tunisia Restaurant was designed by Macro Engineering, the firm that supervised the building of Disneyland.

The Exchange Park building as it was in the mid-1950s. (Photo courtesy of BraniffAirwaysFoundation.org.)

Braniff moved to DFW Airport in 1976 and went bankrupt in 1982. After several owner changes, Exchange Park was sold to the University of Texas Southwestern Medical Center in 2008, where much of the space is offices for UT Southwestern Medical School and Parkland Memorial, but includes retail stores, a bank, a day care center, and other outlets.

THIS USED TO BE: The Braniff Building

NOW IT'S: University of Texas Southwest Medical Center

LOCATION: 6300 Harry Hines Blvd.

West Dallas Finally Connects to Mainstream Dallas

In 2005, West Dallas Investments saw an opportunity for retail development in West Dallas, a part of the city that ran along Singleton Blvd. and ended at the Trinity River. Much of the land they wanted had remained unchanged for decades, with shuttered buildings, aging structures, and most residents barely scraping by. A smelter plant at the corner of Westmoreland Road and Singleton contributed to the neighborhood's blight. A one-time productive warehouse district had become deserted.

Several poor families had owned the West Dallas land for decades, but it had no real value, and they hadn't kept up with ownership records. WDI ran into stumbling blocks looking for landowners, but they persisted. They looked through tax rolls, talked to people in the neighborhood, developed relationships with landowners, and even attended family gatherings, all to gain locals' trust. They had little competition, since the process was burdened with so many headaches. Buying the land proved to be a challenge. The initial 80-acre purchase required 150 transactions.

By the time the adjacent Margaret Hunt Hill Bridge was completed in 2012, WDI was already transforming the longtime warehouse district into a thriving retail apartment enclave called Trinity Groves. The first restaurant was Babb Brothers Barbeque and Blues at 3015 Gulden Ave., which was the longtime home to Strickland Transportation Company. It was followed closely by the gourmet hot dog place Hofman Hots.

With painstaking progress, they reached their goal. Now home to eclectic restaurants, lofts, and shops, Trinity Groves might just be getting started. The vision includes high-rise hotels, office buildings, and apartments. Some think it could even become a second downtown Dallas.

WDI put $45 million into the West Dallas project.

WDI turned a series of abandoned warehouses into a thriving area that might become a second "downtown." (Photo by Harry Hall.)

THIS USED TO BE: An abandoned warehouse district

NOW IT'S: Trinity Groves

LOCATION: At the western end of Margaret Hunt Hill Bridge

Spanish Flu Derails Military Training Camp

For most, the Texas State Fairgrounds conjures images of large crowds, decadent food, exciting rides, next year's car models, and pictures with Big Tex. But a little more than a century ago, Dallas used the area to help with the World War I effort. In 1917, Love Field was formed as an army aviation training facility, and Fair Park was converted into Camp John Dick Aviation Concentration Camp. There, men who had earned their wings were taught the fundamentals and strategy of army discipline. However, Camp Dick proved a challenging environment. Future Hollywood director Preston Sturges, undoubtedly the camp's most famous soldier, wrote about living in sheds meant for animals, saying, "The livestock had been gone for some time, but the powerful former presence haunted the locale like a poltergeist." Their situation improved when the men secured lumber and built floors to sleep on. They also battled the Texas heat. In the summer, they climbed to the roller-coaster apex in search of a cooling breeze.

Famed Hollywood director Preston Sturges wrote that among other problems at Camp Dick, half of the soldiers in the aviation section were enlisted men and half were cadets. The cadets were made officers and made $100 a month; the enlisted men made $33. (Photo by Preston Sturges: His Life in His Words)

But the soldiers' greatest enemy was the Spanish flu, which in 1918 wiped out millions throughout Europe before making its way through North America. As the sickness hit the soldiers, the camp surgeon ordered all incoming men placed in quarantine until they were declared free of influenza. Those returning to their post from official business were required to have their throats sprayed with argyrols, an antiseptic originally developed to prevent gonorrheal blindness in newborns.

St. Paul Hospital pitched 45 tents to care for the large number of sick soldiers at Camp Dick, and new soldiers were quarantined. The flu killed

The entry to the Texas State Fairgrounds, aka Camp Dick, July 6, 1918. (University of Washington Libraries, Special Collections PH Coll 540.6-102.)

Fair Park entry in October 2016. In its first year, 1886, the Texas State Fair attracted 100,000 people. Today, the fair offers visitors a variety of entertainment choices, including dog shows, craft fairs, and the Texas-OU football game, "The Red River Rivalry." (Photo by Nicolas Henderson, https://creativecommons.org/licenses/by/2.0/legalcode.)

between 50 and 100 million worldwide. Dallas reported about 270 deaths per 100,000 residents. The War ended in November 1918, and Camp Dick closed in January 1919. The Texas State Fair was canceled in 1918, but the next year it was called the "Victory Fair."

Director Preston Sturges's 1941 film *Sullivan's Travels* was the inspiration for the 2000 film *O Brother, Where Art Thou?*

THIS USED TO BE: Camp John Dick Aviation Concentration Camp

NOW IT'S: The Texas State Fairgrounds

LOCATION: 3921 Martin Luther King Blvd.

Dallas Welcomes the Fair Park Fire Station

When Dallas's Fair Park Fire Station opened in 1907, locals immediately welcomed their new neighbors, treating them to a housewarming party that included bringing the firemen flowers, fruit, and other treats. The neighborhood addition proved so popular that men vowed to keep the station open one evening a week for visitation. The station became a social and meeting point for the community.

Dallas's first fire station was a two-story, 63-by-80-foot structure staffed with 12 firefighters, five horses, a hose wagon, and a hook-and-ladder truck. The outer wall featured a mottled gray-faced brick on the street sides and red brick on the rear and side. The first floor housed feed rooms, five 10-by-13-foot stalls for the horses, fuel rooms, a workroom with tools, and a work bench for the repair of horses' harnesses. The truck and wagon each faced a high, outward-swinging double door. The second floor included firemen housing, a living room, a large bathroom, the chiefs' office, and a locker room. Horses were phased out in the 1920s. Later, an electronic "joker" notification system allowed the electronic communication of messages and alarms to the firemen through punched paper tape.

After 68 years, in 1975 the Fair Park Fire Station was selected as the site for a new firefighters' museum. It honors the fallen heroes, preserves the firefighting heritage, and offers a variety of education programs for parents, teachers, and children. The museum receives about 5,000 visitors annually, about 60% being children. It preserves the history of firefighting in Dallas through professional quality, restoration, and the display of 2,000 pieces of memorabilia and artifacts. The most popular is "Old Tige," one of only three remaining horse-drawn steam pumper fire engines in the United States that served Dallas from 1884 to 1920.

Today as the FireFighter Museum, the Fair Park Fire Station was remodeled back to its original 1907 facade. (Above) Old Tige, probably the museum's biggest attraction. It pumped 600 gallons of water per minute. (Photos courtesy of the Dallas Firefighter Museum.)

The FPFS was the first horse hospital in Dallas. It even offered loaner animals.

THIS USED TO BE: Fair Park Fire Station
NOW IT'S: The Firefighters Museum
LOCATION: 3801 Parry Ave.

Hotel St. Germain Sets the Standard for Excellence

All seven rooms in Hotel St. Germain are suites, and they include canopied feather beds and fireplaces. Some have Jacuzzis. The most popular room is Number 7, which features a Napoleon bed and a sitting room.

When John Patrick Murphy built what would become Hotel St. Germain a little more than 100 years ago, the three-story, white Queen Anne-style house probably didn't stand out much. It was part of Millionaire's Row, the most desirable part of Dallas that stretched through the 2500 block of Maple. Murphy was a captain for the Confederates in the Civil War, and he had the house built in 1906. His daughter married into the Locke family, and they lived there through the 1960s. After that, the house served as an art gallery, computer school, and a bar.

Since 1991, Claire Heymann has owned and operated Hotel St. Germain as a boutique bed and breakfast. The hotel is named for Heymann's French grandmother and Germaine, the patron saint of Paris. The early 20th-century home is regarded as one of the finest hotel restaurants in the country. Jackets and ties are required for evening dining, and whispering is preferred. Guests have included Prince Albert of Monaco, Oscar de la Renta, and Martha Stewart.

Dining at Hotel St. Germain is done on tables covered with linen cloths, antique Limoges china, and fine crystal wine glasses. *D Magazine* honored the hotel's place setting as having "Best Silverware." The eight-course meal is $85 (without wine, tax, or tip) with a limited selection, but it includes such fare as maple-glazed antelope and herb-crusted filet of beef. Orders must be placed at least 24 hours in advance.

Dining tables are adorned with lavender roses.

Owner Claire Heymann says that unlike most hotels that do the lion's share of business with-out-of-town guests on weekdays, Hotel St. Germain gets a lot of locals on weekends. "Hopefully, when they arrive, it's like being in a different location," she says. (Photo by Harry Hall.)

THIS USED TO BE: A private home
NOW IT'S: Hotel St. Germain
LOCATION: 2516 Maple Ave.

Doak Walker Plaza Honors a Legend

The pedestrian lane on the Southern Methodist University campus that begins just off Binkley Ave. and runs south has an inviting, leisurely feel. Neatly trimmed trees systematically line each side of the 30-foot-wide lane, along with flowers, lights, and benches. Several small, red SMU signs give it a clean look and a sense of pride. At the end of the path, on the northeast corner of Gerald R. Ford Football Stadium, are statues of mustangs, SMU's mascot. Surrounded by the track, Dedman Center, and Armstrong Commons is Doak Walker Plaza. There, on a round raised platform with red flowers at the entry, stands a nine-foot-high statue of a football player in a running pose, wearing a helmet with no face mask.

At the statue's base is an engraving: Doak Walker, 1927–1998. On the base's adjacent corner, a plaque lists Walker's many athletic achievements: four-time Southwest Conference selection, three-time All-American, Cotton Bowl MVP, and other accolades.

Walker personified Jack Armstrong, the All-American Boy of 1940s popular culture. He never drank anything stronger than milk, and he regularly attended Sunday school. And the Mustangs could count on him to come through on the gridiron. In the 1947–48 season, Walker led them to a record of 18-1-3.

Walker played and excelled at running back, defensive back, and kicker. In 1948, he became the first junior to win college football's highest honor, the Heisman Trophy. In 2007, ESPN named Walker number four on the all-time list of greatest players in college football history. Since 1990, college football has given the nation's top running back the Doak Walker Award, named in his honor.

Walker also lettered in baseball and basketball for the Mustangs.

What was once a road that ran through the SMU campus is now a shrine to one who honored SMU and Dallas on and off the field. Doak Walker is still considered one of the all-time college greats. (Photo: Carol M. Highsmith/Library of Congress.)

THIS USED TO BE: Airline Rd.

NOW IT'S: Doak Walker Plaza

LOCATION: NE corner of Gerald R. Ford Football Stadium, SMU campus

The Unlikely Revival of the Filter Building

On the southwest corner of White Rock Lake stand three structures that make up the White Rock Boathouse Facilities: the Sam S. Leake Boathouse, home to boats of three rowing programs; the 1930s-era art deco-style Boomerang, which houses and launches club boats; and the Filter Building, which was included in a 2007 boathouse facilities restoration of $2.5 million. It preserved the Filter Building's urban industrial 1920s style, with exposed red brick walls, original iron trusses, and multiple windows, resulting in a breathtaking view of the lake. The upgrade returned life to a long-abandoned building that once brought life to Dallas.

In 1910, a growing Dallas needed to solve its water shortage problem. In what was then northeast Dallas, White Rock Creek was dammed, farms were dredged, and White Rock Lake became the main water source for East Dallas. The water was pumped directly into the city supply with no filtering or chlorination. Unfortunately, the lake became a victim of its own popularity. Hunting, swimming, and even construction of city-approved cheap homes contributed to a decline in water quality. By 1915, locals were advised to boil lake water before drinking it. As a solution, the Filter Building and Sedimentation Basins were built near the dam. There, an extensive filtering process separated pollutants and sediment from the water. This worked for years until the creation of other lakes, making White Rock unnecessary for drinking. The Filter Building closed, its doors and windows bricked shut.

The renovated Filter Building can now be rented for weddings, parties, and reunions. It has 2,000 square feet of rental space and can accommodate 250 people. A portion of the Filter Building's net revenue supports the White Rock Boathouse outreach and rowing programs, which are geared to both high school athletes and adults.

Although White Rock Lake was once a valuable part of Dallasites' water purification system, other lakes supplanted it for drinking water. For decades, the Filter Building sat dormant and deteriorated. Today's upgraded Filter Building is frequently booked for corporate events and weddings. (Photo by Harry Hall.)

At the end of each rowing season, one or two junior rowers receive the $1,000 John and Anne Mullen Scholarship.

THIS USED TO BE: The Filter Building and Sedimentation Basins

NOW IT'S: The Filter Building on White Rock Lake

LOCATION: 2810 White Rock Lake Rd.

Farmers Market District: Symbol of Dallas Growth

On any day, Dallas's Farmers Market District teems with activity. The area that encompasses South Pearl, Harwood, Marilla, and Cadiz Streets has seen the early days of Dallas and grown with it. What started haphazardly as a few farmers' wagons filled with vegetables and livestock has become one of the city's "can't miss" institutions.

Early Dallas settlers discovered areas of fertile ground, and many farmers grew bounties beyond their needs. They loaded up their carts and set up shop at various places throughout the city, with many commonly settling on Cadiz St. The Farmers Market was named and officially set up in 1941, where farmers sold fruits, vegetables, and livestock such as pigs and goats.

Throughout the decades, the market exploded in popularity. Today, the district includes The Market, a 26,000-square-foot food hall with

restaurants, specialty foods, food artisans, and indoor and outdoor seating. The main attraction is probably The Shed, a climate-controlled, indoor selling spot that holds all kinds of events, including cooking demonstrations. One restaurant is Mudhen Meat and Greens, which has been named Dallas's "Best Farm to Table Restaurant." The Harvest and Taylor Lofts complete the district's landscape.

They even have a Veggie Valet, who will hold your purchases while you bring your car around to pick them up.

The Farmers Market District has something for everyone. And don't worry about asking, "I wonder if it's open?" The Farmers Market is open every day, even Christmas Day.

The district offers an entrepreneurship and farmer program for kids under the age of 14.

The Farmers Market has grown from an informal gathering of local farmers selling what was beyond their needs from the back of their trucks to a major marketing area where vendors teach cooking classes and host arts and crafts vendors through the year. (Photo on opposite page: The Farmers Market of Dallas by Drumguy8800 Creative Commons Attribution-Share Alike 3.0 Unported license. Modern photo by Drumguy 8800 https://creativecommons.org/licenses/by-sa/3.0/deed.en. Vintage photo courtesy of Dallas (Tex.). [Scene at Dallas Farmers Market], photograph, [1950..1959]; https://texashistory.unt.edu/ark:/67531/metapth118021/m1/1/?q=Farmers%20Market%20Dallas%20 1950-1959: accessed August 29, 2019, University of North Texas Libraries, The Portal to Texas History, https://texashistory.unt.edu; crediting Dallas Municipal Archives.)

THIS USED TO BE: Farmers Market

NOW IT'S: Farmers Market District

LOCATION: Area between Pearl Expressway, Marilla, S. Harwood.

The Sportatorium: Host of Pro Wrestling and the King of Rock 'n' Roll

"On TV, the Sportatorium looked like the greatest show on earth. It was literally just a sheet of tin surrounding wooden benches with no backs. It was so ramshackle that when it rained, the water would literally run down the aisles. There was no insulation or air-conditioning. It was the worst arena in Texas." said Gary Hart, professional wrestling booking manager.

Wrestling fans who often overpacked the arena at 1000 S. Industrial Blvd. in the 1970s and 1980s probably preferred the choking cigarette smoke and stale beer smell that came to define the Sportatorium. Built as part of the Texas 1936 Centennial Celebration, it originally hosted top musical performers. Johnny Cash, Chuck Berry, and even Elvis Presley performed there.

Elvis Presley at the Sportatorium, 1955. (Courtesy of Steve Bonner.)

However, in Sportatorium history, they are viewed as warm-up acts. Professional wrestlers became the real stars. The athletes knew their fan base, and they didn't disappoint. Bill Curry defeated Danny McShain for the professional association's Brass Knuckles Championship. Fritz Von Erich once hit another wrestler with a wooden chair, creating a gash that required 30 stitches. Two local TV stations broadcast matches at the same time and claimed that 7,000 sometimes packed the 5,000-seat arena. Professional wrestling reached a fever pitch when Von Erich's sons Kerry, David, and Kevin became international stars in large part because of their massive popularity at the Sportatorium.

Ultimately, in the 1990s the arena lost its audience, and fire destroyed it in 2000. David Shoemaker wrote in *Squared Circle: Life, Death, and Professional Wrestling*, "The wrestling crowds had diminished to the point that it hardly seemed necessary."

The Sportatorium's remnants were demolished in 2003.

Sportatorium today. (Top photos courtesy of Steve Bonner. Bottom photo by Harry Hall.)

Before the Sportatorium was famous for wrestling, it was a music venue that saw some of the greatest acts through the 1950s, like Johnny Cash, Elvis, and Carl Perkins (pictured), playing from an open wrestling ring. The lot where it once stood has been for sale for years.

While closing one night, concessionaire Ed McLemore lifted a man he found slumped over a chair and found a knife protruding from between his shoulder blades.

THIS USED TO BE: The Sportatorium
NOW IT'S: Ft. Worth Promotions, Inc
LOCATION: 1000 S. Industrial Blvd.

The One-Time Coffin Company Now Offers Luxury

In the mid-19th century, when caskets were still known as *coffins*—that is, all wood and made by a carpenter—and funeral directors were called *undertakers*, family and friends typically took care of a recently deceased relative. A coffin was sent to the family's home and then later taken to the cemetery. During the Civil War, improvements in embalming meant bodies could last longer, dramatically changing the burial process.

In 1908, Joseph Parks founded the five-story Dallas Coffin Company in downtown Dallas near what is now Dealey Plaza. The business would be a sort of a one-stop shop for funeral directors, carrying coffins, caskets, hearses, and all types of mortuary needs. Funeral directors contacted the company 24/7 by telephone or telegraph. Orders were shipped by express rail.

The next year, possibly motivated by the massive 1908 flood that wiped out much of western downtown Dallas, Parks moved to 1325 South Lamar St. The new building's exterior consisted of clay tile and red brick with double-hung wood windows on the east, south, and north sides of the building and metal windows on the west side. Administration offices made up the first floor, while sales and the finishing of coffins and caskets operated on the next four.

The company went out of business in the late 1940s. The building passed through decades of occupancy and vacancy. Sears bought it to expand its catalogue and retail operations but vacated the building in the 1980s. A developer purchased it in 2010 to transform the building from a warehouse into the NYLO Hotel. On February 28, 2019, Dallas was introduced to the CANVAS Hotel, billed as "Dallas's newest boutique hotel experience," where for one night at least, guests can rest in peace.

The Dallas Coffin Company has had many identities over its 100-year-plus existence, but probably its greatest renovation took place in 2010, when a developer converted it from a warehouse into the NYLO Hotel. (Photo: Dallas Coffin Company Building in Dallas, https://creativecommons.org/licenses/by-sa/4.0/deed.en. Photographer: Renelibrary.)

Stay one night in a CANVAS loft and get a $25 food credit to either Chef's Palette or Gallery Rooftop Lounge.

THIS USED TO BE: Dallas Coffin Company
NOW IT'S: CANVAS Hotel
LOCATION: 1325 S. Lamar St.

The Southwest's Greatest Playground

Several curious artifacts are seen on the northwest corner of Lake Cliff Park. Steps lead from the pond to nowhere: an awkward-looking aging sidewalk and a dormant, rusting fountain.

That is about the only physical evidence of an ambitious early 20th century project that, for a few years, Dallas leaders hoped would bring unparalleled entertainment to Oak Cliff.

They called it "the Southwest's Greatest Playground."

Today, Lake Cliff Park is nestled in Oak Cliff, just far enough from downtown Dallas to give it an atmosphere of serenity. It offers what you'd expect from a park: a tennis court, softball diamond, playground, and open-air covered picnic tables. That tranquility belies the excitement that was the dream of some of Dallas's city leaders.

Charles Mangold and a group of prominent businessmen bought 50 acres of land near Zang and Colorado to turn Oak Cliff into a family entertainment destination they hoped would rival America's largest amusement park, New York's Coney Island.

In summer 1906, they introduced Dallas to a spectacle that included a pool, waterslides, a skating rink billed as "The World's Largest," and three theaters, each one reserved for what many considered a novelty—moving pictures.

Other attractions included appearances by nationally known vaudevillians such as Al Jolson, and hot-air balloons that frequently featured parachutists and trapeze artists who would perform aerial shows as they descended.

The park proved popular until the flood of 1908, which wiped out the bridges that brought in patrons from Dallas to Oak Cliff.

A new bridge was erected, but it was too late for Southwest Park. Citing financial strains, Mangold sold most of the land back to the city. Many of the buildings and rides were relocated.

Hand-painted postcard: "Beautiful Lake Cliff. The Greatest Amusement Park in the Southwest." Printed ca. 1906–1913 by C. Weichsel Company. George W. Cook Dallas/Texas Image Collection. (Courtesy of DeGoyler Library, Southern Methodist University.)

On July 5, 1908, the *Dallas Morning News* reported that 12,000 people "swarmed through the gates at Lake Cliff Park last night."

THIS USED TO BE: The Southwest's Greatest Playground

NOW IT'S: Lake Cliff Park

LOCATION: 1200 N. Zang Blvd.

Interurban Building (page 152)

(Photo by Harry Hall.)

The Belmont Hotel (page 54)
(Photo by Harry Hall.)

Dallas World Aquarium (page 174)

(Photo by Steven Carlton, https://creativecommons.org/licenses/by/2.0.)

Pachanga Wholesale Bridal & Quinceañera (page 44)

(Photo by Harry Hall.)

Big Tex (page 14)

(Photo by Christian Bradford, Creative Commons 2.0.)

Santa Fe Building (page 162)

(Photo by Harry Hall.)

Sons of Hermann Hall (page 60)
(Photo by Nicolas Henderson, Creative Commons 2.0.)

Firefighters Museum (page 72)

(Courtesy of the Firefighters Museum.)

Lake Cliff Park (page 86)

(Photo by Harry Hall.)

Frogtown (page 140)

(Photo courtesy of www.visitdallas.com.)

Dallas County Administration Building (page 22)

(Photo by Dakota L., from Wikipedia, https://creativecommons.org/licenses/by-sa/4.0.)

Tootsies (page 134)

(Photo by Harry Hall.)

Ambassador Hotel (page 168)

(Photo by Harry Hall.)

This Gas Station Housed a Killer

Most of West Dallas is populated with a small series of seemingly struggling businesses and lower-rent housing. Included in the neighborhood at 1221 Singleton Boulevard is a long-neglected, brown-brick abandoned gas station with a small wooden room added to the back. The roof is shot, and the door and windows are covered with "burglar bars." The "No Trespassing" and "Private Property" signs seem almost comical under the circumstances.

In the early 1920s, this site was the home of the Barrow family, most notably that of the future notorious bank robber and killer Clyde Barrow. When Clyde was 12 years old, his father Henry Basil got enough money to leave the tenant farmer business and buy a Star Service Station on what was then Eagle Ford Road. As the elder Barrow ran the business, the family, which would eventually include seven children, lived in the back room.

From 1926 to 1930, Clyde and his older brother Marvin "Buck" Barrow were arrested several times for robbing stores and stealing cars. After Clyde's release from prison in late 1930, he took up company with a woman he'd met and fallen in love with earlier that year—the already-married 20-year-old Bonnie Parker. The couple grew famous and infamous for robbing and murdering; they were dubbed "Public Enemy #1" by FBI Director J. Edgar Hoover. On May 23, 1934, in Bienville Parish, Louisiana, they were executed in a hail of gunfire.

The Barrow family sold the gas station in the 1940s and eventually went through several owners. No marker acknowledges its historical significance. Recently, the real estate development company Oaxaca Interests bought the Barrow Gas Station that was once home to Clyde Barrow. Its future is unknown.

The station's front door is missing but gated, allowing the curious to take pictures of the inside.

In 1938, four years after Bonnie and Clyde were gunned down, a West Dallas hoodlum named S. J. "Baldy" Whatley threw a Molotov cocktail on the gas station roof. Another time, he drove by and fired shotgun blasts into the station, injuring Clyde's 65-year-old mother and costing her an eye. For that crime, Whatley got 12 years for aggravated assault. (Photo on left: Courtesy of Texas Hideout Tripod. Photo on right: Courtesy of Robin Hollenkamp Keyboard Basket.)

THIS USED TO BE: Home of Clyde Barrow
NOW IT'S: An abandoned gas station
LOCATION: 1221 Singleton Blvd.

Arts Magnet School Earns National Acclaim

Booker T. Washington High School for the Performing and Visual Arts (aka Arts Magnet) might be the only high school in America to produce multiple Grammy Award winners and a baseball Hall of Famer who also won the Presidential Medal of Freedom, Ernie Banks. In addition, the school has produced professional dancers, actors, producers, many other arts-related performers, and 13 Presidential Scholars.

The school, now located in the heart of Dallas's popular Arts District, didn't start as a major player for gifted artists. Its history goes back to 1892, at the southeast corner of Hall and Cochran Streets, where it made history by fielding the state's first football team in 1900. In 1911, it was named Dallas Colored High School. In 1922, the school moved to its current location and was renamed Booker T. Washington High School. It kept variations of that name for the next several decades.

In 1976, a desegregation order created the Arts Magnet School, revamping the curriculum that emphasizes gifted students with potential for careers in the arts. The school has no football, basketball, or cheerleaders. (Ironically, when Banks graduated in 1950, it didn't have a baseball team, either.) Today, it boasts a more diverse student body, and its approximately 150 annual graduates earn between $1.5 and $8.5 million in academic and artistic scholarships.

In 2008, a new Washington facility was completed at a cost of $65 million. The original building, now a historic landmark, has been preserved.

The school produced five Grammy Award winners: Norah Jones, Erykah Badu, Edie Brickell, the gospel group God's Property, and trumpeter Roy Hargrove.

The main building is all that's left of the 1922 version of Booker T. Washington High School. Originally called Dallas Colored High School, it sat on the southeast corner of Hall and Cochran Streets. It was also home to the state's first high school football team. (Photo on bottom: Creative Commons Modern Building, https://creativecommons.org/licenses/by/3.0/deed.en, photographer Andreas Praefcke. Photo on top: https://creativecommons.org/licenses/by-sa/3.0/deed.en, photographer: Drumguy8800.)

THIS USED TO BE: Dallas Colored High School

NOW IT'S: Booker T. Washington High School for the Performing Arts

LOCATION: 2501 Flora St.

The Brothers Who Redefined the Retail Industry

Since 1966, El Centro College, a member of the Hispanic-serving Institution and the Hispanic Association of Colleges and Universities, has stood at the corner of 801 Main Street in the center of downtown. The building is an example of the Chicago School of commercial architecture, featuring large windows and Sullivanesque terra-cotta ornamentation. The school offers career training in more than 50 fields, and their degree plans specialize in medical and technology fields such as nursing, culinary and fashion design, and marketing.

Originally, El Centro was the Sanger Brothers building, one of Dallas's first retailers, opening in 1872, the same year the railroad appeared. While the Sanger Brothers did have quality merchandise and dry goods such as clothes, hats, and shoes, they might have created what is now called "the enhanced customer experience." The innovative brothers offered first-in-the-state conveniences such as electricity, telephones, and passenger elevators. Customers could place orders by mail, and beginning in 1879, Dallas deliveries were free. They began extending credit and using mortgages as collateral, resulting in the brothers acquiring considerable land and property.

In 1965, the company reportedly turned down an offer to build a store in the new climate-controlled North Park Mall, and the spot was taken by Neiman Marcus.

Unfortunately, after Alex, the last surviving founding Sanger brother, died in 1925, the company suffered through a decades-long decline. A series of reorganizations and sales failed. In 1987, 21 years after the downtown store became part of El Centro, Sangers was sold to Federated Department Stores, who changed the name to Foley's.

Among the Sanger Brothers's early salesmen were bank robber Frank James and Neiman Marcus founder Herbert Marcus.

The Sanger Brothers/El Centro Building is the only surviving Lang and Witchell-designed commercial structure in Dallas. Started in 1905, the firm would become Dallas's most prestigious architectural firm, designing several structures that appear on the National Register of Historic Places, including this one, which made the NRHP list in 1975. (Photo by RadicalBender at English Wikipedia, https://creativecommons.org/licenses/by-sa/3.0/deed.en.)

THIS USED TO BE: Sanger Brothers

NOW IT'S: El Centro College

LOCATION: 801 Main St.

When Blacks and Whites Lived in Different Worlds

Forest High School, an Italian Renaissance-style building, was built in 1916 in Fair Park, then a premier whites-only school in one of Dallas's fastest growing areas. The school graduated some notable students, including television producer Aaron Spelling (class of '20) and retail mogul Stanley Marcus (class of '40). After World War II, the demographics began changing, with an increasing number of Blacks moving into the area. Since segregation was still part of the city's educational landscape, something needed to give.

On June 14, 1956, Dallas school trustees made what was literally a black-and-white decision. The board redrew the boundary lines, officially making the school exclusively for Blacks, and changed the school name to James Madison High School. The move helped to preserve segregation and relieved overcrowding by two other growing Black-exclusive high schools, Lincoln and Booker T. Washington. Forest's white and Jewish students were transferred to Crozier Tech, and many resented the reassignment. Then the school's principal declared that all trophies and other school-themed memorabilia would follow the students to their new school. Students and school-sponsored organizations signed a petition that the Forest name, the green-and-white colors, and lion mascot be preserved for any new all-white school that might be built. Madison is the Mighty Trojans, and its colors are green and gold. In 1981, the street address switched from Forest Avenue to Martin Luther King Jr. Blvd.

Notable Madison graduates include Dave Stallworth, who won an NBA championship with the New York Knicks; Sylvia Stanfield, the first Black female US ambassador to Brunei; and Dwight White, a member of the Pittsburgh Steelers Steel Curtain defense.

Both Madison and Crozier Tech (Dallas High School) have been declared Dallas landmarks and are listed in the National Register of Historic Places.

Although the schools were segregated, at least one Forest High graduate said that the white students from Forest frequently played sandlot football with the Black kids from nearby Lincoln High School (many of whom would transfer to Madison). "There were never any fights or anything like that," he said. "They'd play hard." James Madison High School, formerly Forest Avenue High School. (Photographer: Renelibrary https://creativecommons.org/licenses/by-sa/3.0/deed.en.)

In the 2018-19 school year, 59% of Madison's students were Black, and 39% were Hispanic.

THIS USED TO BE: Forest Avenue High School
NOW IT'S: James Madison High School
LOCATION: 3000 Martin L. King Jr. Blvd.

The Theater That Wouldn't Stay Down

Edwin and Lisa Cabaniss had been eyeing Oak Cliff's abandoned Kessler Theater for several years. In 2009, they made the purchase. After 17 months of extensive renovation, the Kessler Theater reopened on March 18, 2010, as a live music venue. The skeleton staff worked for little pay, and acts worked for gate percentages instead of a standard fee. The cost-cutting strategy worked. Since then, it has become a vital part of a recent area revitalization that includes other nearby landmarks, the Texas Theatre, and the Bishop Arts District.

The Kessler Theater probably shouldn't exist. When it was built in 1942 in Oak Cliff at the corner of West Davis Street and Clinton Avenue, the pre-war, art deco-style building got off to a great start showing movies. Dewey Groom and the Texas Longhorns performed live between weekend matinees, playing their form of Texas swing music for what they called the "Hay Loft series." In 1945, the Kessler was sold and became part of Gene "the Singing Cowboy" Autry's theater chain. It was sold again in 1952. Then came decades of tragedy and inactivity that would have ended most facilities. In 1957, it took a direct hit from a tornado. Renovated as the Revival Tabernacle in 1962, it was destroyed by a three-alarm fire. Later, it briefly served as an embroidery company.

It took the Cabanisses to recapture the Kessler's earlier magic.

Although the Kessler seats only 800, it offers a kitchen and a fully stocked bar of beers, wine, and spirits. In 2011, the Oak Cliff Chamber of Commerce named it "Business of the Year." It has also won several "Best Music Venue" and "Best Performing Arts Center" awards.

Grammy-winning singer Marc Cohn says, "Kessler is one of my new favorite venues to play."

The Kessler is also home to Lisa's Children's Ballet School and hosts private events.

The Kessler has a resilient history after taking a direct hit from a tornado in 1957, a three-alarm fire in the 1960s, and decades of abandonment to become an award-winning musical arena. (Photo by Michael Barera, https://creativecommons.org/licenses/by-sa/4.0/deed.en.)

THIS USED TO BE: Kessler Theater (showed movies)
NOW IT'S: Kessler Theater (music venue)
LOCATION: 1230 W. Davis

Old Mill Restaurant Maintains Nostalgic Character

The Old Mill Restaurant stands in Fair Park at the northwest corner of Grand and 1st Avenue within eyeshot of both the automobile building and Big Tex. Built in 1936 as the Old Mill Inn for the Texas Centennial Exposition, it illustrated how far Texas had progressed since winning its freedom from Mexico 100 years earlier. The mill was a recreation of the Burris Flour Mill that once stood in McKinney, Texas, and some of the original mill's timbers were used in the replica. German carpenters re-laid the roof, laying hand-carved beams secured with wooded pegs. The rustic exterior, a working water wheel, and fountains were duplicated features of the original mill. Inside, the atmosphere from a longtime past is highlighted with a fireplace that is still in its original state from 1936.

When it opened, women from all over North Texas came to the mill to watch Ida Chitwood give cooking demonstrations in her model test kitchen, which frequently saw her using new cooking techniques.

Now an eatery, the Old Mill Inn Restaurant is open only for lunch every day, with special hours in the fall during the three-week run of the State Fair. (Note: The restaurant deals in cash, not fair coupons.) The menu includes Southern favorites like chicken-fried steak, sandwich baskets, and desserts. It is now available for meetings and private events, such as weddings. On Fridays and Saturdays, a limited number of patrons can dine upstairs and enjoy Keith and Margo's Murder Mystery Texas, PG-13-rated plays that encourage attendees to "dine, drink, deduce, dance, and die laughing!

The inn once displayed a Borden Dairy exhibit that included a real Elsie the Cow and Elmer the Bull.

In 1936, the Old Mill Restaurant, then established as the Old Mill Inn, was similar in design to an actual mill built 100 years earlier, including German carpenters securing beams with wooden pegs. Note the water wheel behind the Old Mill sign. (Photo by Michael Barera, https://creativecommons.org/licenses/by-sa/4.0/deed.en.)

THIS USED TO BE: Old Mill Inn, a replica of an 1836 flour mill

NOW IT'S: Old Mill Inn Restaurant

LOCATION: 3611 Grand Ave.

America's Most Decorated Soldier Owned This Farmhouse

Before the 1930s-era farmhouse at what is now at the 14000 block of Midway Road became Dovie's Restaurant, it belonged to First Lieutenant Audie Murphy, Hollywood actor and the nation's most decorated war hero. The far north part of Dallas that once made up that block of Midway Road is gone. Now part of Addison, the area bustles with activity, with cars constantly whizzing by and seemingly endless rows of restaurants. Only the farmhouse has remained the same.

The two-story, brown-and-cream brick house dominated by long, narrow windows on both sides sits about 100 yards from the main street, hidden by distance and red brick, Colonial-style office buildings. Outside the addition of a courtyard, the house's exterior has remained virtually the same. However, the four upstairs bedrooms were converted into dining areas and a bar. It featured three wood-burning fireplaces and a dance floor, and it could serve more than 200. The restaurant served traditional American fare.

Born in Kingston, Texas, Murphy enlisted in World War II and earned virtually all military honors possible, including the Medal of Honor and Distinguished Service Cross, plus honors from Belgium and France. From 1948 to 1969, he starred in more than 40 feature films and one television series. In the early 1950s, Murphy married Pamela Archer and bought the farmhouse, where the two planned to eventually settle down.

The Murphys lived in California and never moved to the farmhouse. Murphy died in a plane crash in 1971. Dovie's closed in 2016.

Audie Murphy's grave at Arlington National Cemetery is the second most visited, behind that of President Kennedy.

Built in the early 1930s, this one-time farmhouse was once owned by America's most decorated soldier, Audie Murphy. He intended to live there, but he never did. It was turned into Dovie's Restaurant in 1980. It has since closed and is slowly deteriorating. (Photo by Harry Hall.)

THIS USED TO BE: A farmhouse, purchased by Audie Murphy

NOW IT'S: Closed Dovie's Restaurant

LOCATION: 14671 Midway Rd.

A Tragedy That Transformed the World's Health

Since the 1940s, the Nichols family lived in a mansion that stood almost alone at the corner of Willow Lane and Preston Road, with white bricks and a seven-columned facing creating a pastoral setting against nearby cotton fields, crepe myrtles, and ponds stocked for fishing and home to many ducks.

After Clarice Nichols's husband died from a heart attack at age 57, she turned the tragedy into an avenue to increasing people's length and quality of life. In 1969, Clarice accepted an offer to sell their family home to a doctor whom she had heard speak on the value of cardiovascular health. He wanted to use the Nichols home to establish an office to focus his practice on a revolutionary idea—preventative medicine.

The buyer was Dr. Kenneth Cooper, an Air Force physician who had just published *Aerobics*, a groundbreaking book on the benefits of exercise. It would sell 30 million copies and be translated into 41 languages.

Since its opening as the Cooper Institute in 1970, the Cooper Aerobics Center has expanded from a two-story doctor's office to become the world's premier research center for studying the positive effects of exercise.

At age 22, Houston Nichols, who grew up in the mansion, received his first physical in what was once his parents' bedroom. "It was a thorough exam for the time," he said, "and I passed."

When Dr. Kenneth Cooper bought the Nichols Mansion in 1969, it sat alone and included a pond that attracted ducks. Clarice Nichols would sell only on the condition that the mansion would remain intact and the ducks could stay. (Modern photo by Harry Hall. Nichols Mansion: Courtesy of the Cooper Institute.)

Today the facility has grown to 30 acres and has expanded into five divisions: the Cooper Clinic, the Institute, fitness center, spa, and hotel. In addition, it offers its fitness center members walking trails, a swimming pool, and tennis courts. The center's greatest influence has been in determining exercise standards for a variety of populations, mostly by following and studying the exercise and fitness habits of more than 110,000 people for more than five decades.

THIS USED TO BE: Nichols Mansion
NOW IT'S: Cooper Aerobics Center
LOCATION: 12200 Preston Rd.

Attention-Getting Billboard

Sydney, Australia has the Opera House; Paris, the Eiffel Tower; and in New York City, everyone wants to visit the Statue of Liberty. Notable landmarks are generally buildings or structures that become tourist attractions or give pride to the area. One of Dallas's landmarks is a billboard.

Thousands of daily commuters and tourists see the billboard standing high on Goat Hill adjacent to Stemmons Frwy. just north of downtown. Each day, 1.5 million gallons of water flows 45 feet over artificial waterproof rocks and has been doing so since Dallas-based Tracy-Locke created it in 1956. Over the years, it advertised a variety of products, mostly cigarettes or alcohol, including Absolut Vodka and its original subject, Pearl Beer.

Stories abound about the billboard's base being a target of fun-seekers, such as college kids holding skinny-dipping parties, detergent bombings, and adding orange or red dye during Texas-OU weekend. The most intriguing might be the doctor who somehow lost his $15,000 Cartier watch in the waterfall basin. The diver hired to retrieve it said the doctor gave specific orders that the watch be returned to his office and not his home.

In 2008, Dallas declared the billboard an "extraordinarily significant sign," and Rock-Scrapes gave the aging symbol a facelift that included removing the digital time and temperature display, and a new, taller fence to discourage trespassers such as college kids and doctors.

After more than 60 years, the waterfall billboard remains one of the most fascinating and eye-catching aspects of Big D. While the sign doesn't have the historical significance of the School Book Depository or the ostentatiousness of the Adolphus Hotel, maybe no other Dallas structure can match it for uniqueness or awesomeness.

In 2013, the *Dallas Morning News* proclaimed the waterfall billboard "the biggest beer sign in the US."

The waterfall billboard is one of the most familiar sights in Dallas. Its location on Stemmons Frwy. means that it's seen and admired by tens of thousands of MetroPlex residents every day. (https://creativecommons.org/licenses/by-sa/4.0/deed.en. Photo by Jrihani.)

THIS USED TO BE: The side of a hill

NOW IT'S: Waterfall Billboard

LOCATION: Goat Hill, just off Stemmons Frwy., north of downtown

Parkland Memorial Hospital Moves Forward

Parkland Memorial Hospital grew from a wooden building in 1894 on a 17-acre plot at Oak Lawn and Maple Avenue to being replaced by the state's first brick hospital in 1913. During the Depression, patient care expanded beyond its traditional base—the indigent. Through the years, Parkland provided better care and more services, such as adding two four-story wings and creating its own blood bank. In 1952, a vastly expanded Parkland moved about a mile to Harry Hines Blvd., where it remained until 2015, when a state-of-the art hospital was completed at a cost of $1.3 billion.

Whatever awards Dallas's Parkland Memorial Hospital wins, no matter what groundbreaking medical mysteries they might uncover, or top doctors they hire, for much of the public, the hospital will probably be most associated with the deaths of President John F. Kennedy, his assassin, Lee Harvey Oswald, and his assassin, Jack Ruby.

The tragedies began on November 22, 1963, when Oswald shot Kennedy. Two days later, during a jail transfer, a stunned nation watched on television as Jack Ruby, a low-rent Dallas club owner and small-time hood, shot and killed Oswald. On January 3, 1967, three weeks after being admitted, a cancer-stricken Ruby also died at Parkland.

Today, the newest version of Parkland Memorial Hospital is a 17-story, 1.7-million-square-foot facility with 862 beds. It has a neonatal intensive care unit, a burn intensive care unit, and advanced imaging. It also sponsors several school-based clinics and outreach and education programs.

Parkland Memorial will never escape its association with the city's darkest episode, but it hasn't let that tragedy define it. The hospital continues to win awards for excellence, such as the 2016 Gage Award for teaching patients to self-administer certain intravenous medications at home, saving time and money.

Parkland Memorial Hospital is one of Dallas's most enduring structures. Since its inception as a wooden hospital in 1894, it's gone through several moves and upgrades. Today, the latest version of Parkland Memorial is large, impressive, modern, and innovative. But no matter what, it will always be associated with Dallas's darkest day. (Photo on previous page: https://texashistory.unt.edu/ark:/67531/metapth599399/: accessed August 30, 2019, University of North Texas Libraries, The Portal to Texas History, https://texashistory.unt.edu; crediting Historic Mesquite, Inc. Photo above: https://creativecommons.org/licenses/by-sa/3.0/deed.en by: Renelibrary. November 22, 1963, Public Domain. Photo on left: Courtesy of Pixabay.)

In 1964, Dr. Paul Peters led a team of Parkland doctors through the state's first successful kidney transplant.

THIS USED TO BE: Parkland, a frame hospital
NOW IT'S: Parkland Memorial Hospital
LOCATION: 5201 Harry Hines

Dallas's First Home

The first home in Dallas was modest—one room measuring just 14 by 15 feet, smaller than the paint area on a basketball court. Features included walls just high enough for a door, an opening for a fireplace, a dirt floor, and no windows. It wasn't much, but when you had one man hewing and creating a home for him and his new wife, using only an ax, it seemed extraordinary. And it was a major upgrade from the lean-to he had been living in since his arrival from Arkansas in 1841.

In 1843, John Neely Bryan, a native of Tennessee and an accomplished trader and adventurer, selected a spot on the east bank near the three forks of the Trinity River and built the first log cabin in what would become Dallas. Three years later, a rising river made the couple's home uninhabitable, and Bryan built another cabin a bit farther from the river. This one was more elaborate, with two rooms separated by a breezeway.

For years, stories circulated about what happened to the original cabin—that it became part of "shacktown," and just dodged being destroyed when an observant Dallasite recognized it—but today the most agreed-upon tale is that the wooden home that stands at 600 Elm Street is a replica erected in the 1930s when a flood destroyed the original. Since 1971, the reconstructed cabin's home has been near the Dallas courthouse, not far from the spot where the founder of Dallas started it all more than 175 years ago.

Bryan's cabin also served as a post office and courthouse.

A replica of Dallas's first structure, built by John Neely Bryan, with an ax as his only tool. He became a true leader in the town's development, including serving as postmaster. (Courtesy of http://lccn.loc.gov/2014632145. Photo by Carol M. Highsmith.)

THIS USED TO BE: Dallas's first structure

NOW IT'S: A museum

LOCATION: 600 Elm St.

A Cook-Off That Inspired an International Restaurant Chain

The 7-Eleven at the corner of Meadow Road and Greenville Avenue doesn't look much different than most of the other 68,000 International Southland Corporation outlets. At a busy intersection, there's never a shortage of customers. The familiar red, white, red, orange, and green banner and 7-Eleven logo offer the usual convenience items, including the company's famous multi-flavored frosty carbonated drink, Slurpees.

This location was once home to the first Chili's restaurant.

Chili's grew from an idea by Dallasite Larry Lavine, who drew inspiration from his father-in-law, race-car driver, and designer Carroll Shelby. Shelby held the first World Championship Chili Cook-Off at Terlingua, Texas, and Lavine saw an opportunity. Modeling two of his childhood favorites, Burger House and Geoff's Hamburgers, Lavine took over a hot dog stand and sold burgers, French fries, and "a bowl of red."

In 1975, he converted a post office at Meadow and Greenville, opening the first Chili's restaurant. He created an atmosphere for a laid-back, full-service, family-friendly dining experience that encouraged conversation. The original Chili's had the familiar green-frame exterior, with many windows trimmed in tan. Inside, the tabletops featured hand-painted Mexican tile work. The walls were covered with Texas-themed photos and—perhaps the customers' favorite—the Texas state flag. Lavine apparently perfected his chili recipe, for the August 1982 edition of *D Magazine* said, "The best chili in Dallas is at Chili's. And best by a wide margin. It's so good that you may find yourself holding onto the table with both hands and stamping your feet on the floor." In 1983, Lavine sold his 23 Chili's restaurants to Norman Brinker. Brinker took Chili's from a regional attraction to a worldwide sensation, with 1,600 stores in 23 countries annually serving 281 million customers.

The corner that was home to two international corporations both revolutionized their respective industries, and both were born in Dallas.

What started in a converted post office turned into one of the most popular restaurant chains in history, with 1,600 eateries in 35 countries. Today, the site of the first Chili's is another Dallas corporate discovery, 7-Eleven. (Photo by Harry Hall.)

Each Chili's in the United States has an upside-down, red-and-green picture hanging in it. The Chinese word for *arrive* rhymes with "upside down."

THIS USED TO BE: The first Chili's restaurant

NOW IT'S: A 7-Eleven

LOCATION: 7567 Greenville Ave.

Has the Continental Gin Building Gone Bust?

The divots in the gravel parking lot and driveway leading into the white Continental Gin Building threaten to bottom out any car. The painted sign reading "Continental Gin Company" across the top story is faded, the dozen or so windows below it bleeding rust. The windows and doors are shuttered. The structure's dock, once one of the country's top cotton processors, is wasting away.

In the late 19th century, while working at his father's cotton gin in Mexia, young Robert Munger saw an opportunity. Growing increasingly frustrated at long lines and a slow ginning process, which contributed to the inability to fill railcars, he set out to find a way to streamline the process.

He developed what became known as system ginning. He replaced animal power with steam, making the cotton flow through the machines more smoothly and quickly. A condenser and screen drum separated the cotton lint and cleaned out dust and other contaminants from the cotton. Munger incorporated conveyor belts and ginned and baled cotton faster than anyone. The cost-saving measures not only worked more efficiently; they produced a higher-quality product.

However, he couldn't interest a local gin manufacturer in his new process, so in 1884, he and other investors moved to Dallas. There, he started the Munger Improved Cotton Machine Manufacturing Company. In 1899, the Munger companies (in Texas and Alabama) merged with others, and they became the largest manufacturer of cotton gins in the United States.

After more than a half century of success, the Cotton Machine Manufacturing Company closed in 1962, becoming an elevator manufacturer. In 1982, the building was converted into an artist studio and lofts, which closed in November 2018 in favor of a planned building renovation that has yet to materialize.

The entrepreneurship of Robert Munger created the Continental Gin Company. Munger improved the ginning process, making it faster and giving a higher-quality product. He had a strong market. In those days, one-sixth of the world's cotton was grown within a 150-mile radius of Dallas. (Vintage photo: Chas. Erwin Arnold, Maker of Finest Photographs, Dallas, TX 1914; part of the George W. Cook Image Collection. Modern photo: Harry Hall.)

Since 1983, the Continental Gin Building has been listed on the National Register of Historic Places.

THIS USED TO BE: The Continental Gin Company
NOW IT'S: Abandoned
LOCATION: 3309 Elm St.

From Old Red Courthouse to Museum

The building commonly referred to as Old Red is appropriately nicknamed, and it's one of the most distinctively designed and enduring structures in town. Its spire-topped turrets give it an appearance of a castle. On top sit four wyverns—Latin for "serpent." The wyverns have two legs, wings, and a spiny back. The red sandstone Richardsonian Romanesque style is the creation of Arkansas architect Max Orlopp of Orlopp & Kusener.

Whether one is new or old to Dallas, just being near it gives a fascinating view into Dallas history. It's located amidst a myriad of Dallas landmarks, such as John Neely Bryan's cabin, Dealey Plaza and the JFK Memorial, the Sixth Floor Museum, and the West End.

Built in 1892, Old Red served as a courthouse until 1966. Today, it's a museum that is home to some of Dallas's most memorable and infamous artifacts, such as the county's first traffic light, the handcuffs that once held Lee Harvey Oswald, and the Stetson worn by Larry Hagman in the TV show *Dallas*.

Also helping to recapture the museum's early courthouse days is the restoration of the court's Grand Staircase. Some segments are restored from the original, which in 1920 was removed in lieu of office space.

In its more than 100-year history, the courthouse has seen a lot of Dallas history. In 1975, it was designated as part of the Dallas Landmark Historic District and List of National Historic Landmarks in Texas, List of Dallas Landmarks, and other honors.

Just after World War II, Old Red's three-ton clock was removed. Supposedly, "when the atmosphere was right," the bell could be heard 10 miles away.

In its early years, the building was acclaimed as "unsurpassed in the grandeur of its architecture, the magnificence of its proportions and the elegance of its finish and appointments" by any other courthouse south of the Mason and Dixon Line." (Photo by Fredlyfish4, courtesy of https://creativecommons.org/licenses/by-sa/4.0/deed.en. December 2014.)

THIS USED TO BE: "Old Red" Courthouse

NOW IT'S: Old Red Museum of Dallas County History and Culture

LOCATION: 100 S. Houston St.

Tootsies Continues Predecessor's High Standards

The Tootsies window showroom at 8300 Preston Road changes with the seasons, but the displays are always contemporary and stylish, whether the selections be shoes, bags, or jewelry. In addition to its fashions, Tootsies is passionate about service, a critical key to success in this neighborhood in Dallas's upscale Highland Park. Their website says, "Every decision we make is based on what our customers desire."

Tootsies is carrying on the philosophy of the retailing innovator it replaced, Neiman Marcus. After 45 years operating out of one downtown store, defining Dallas clothing styles, and almost single-handedly creating an air of catering to a demanding high-class clientele, Neiman Marcus opened a 63,000-square-foot second store in 1951 at Preston Center. Unlike the flagship outlet, this one focused on the culture of the Southwestern Indians, including colors, weaves, paintings, and pottery. One year, to promote new colors in fabric, Stanley Marcus borrowed 20 Gauguin paintings, some of which had never been displayed publicly. In an unintended but thrilling result, area teachers said the exhibit sparked an increased interest in the study of art. Adding to the store's popularity was the famous Neiman Marcus catalog, birthed when newsman Edward R. Murrow asked Stanley what unique Christmas gifts he had in his catalog for 1952.

Seeing an opportunity to expand the brand, in 1965, Marcus took advantage of an offer to move a few miles north to the new Northpark Mall, then the largest climate-controlled shopping center in the world. The Preston Center store closed.

Tootsies has succeeded by working with some of the top designers from the United States and Europe. In addition to the stylish fashions and service, customers can take advantage of an in-house bar.

Tootsies consults with top designers "on both sides of the Atlantic" to give their customers the best and latest in high fashion. (Photo by Harry Hall.)

The Neiman Marcus catalog grew in popularity and reportedly became the most stolen item from residential mailboxes.

THIS USED TO BE: Neiman Marcus's second store

NOW IT'S: Tootsies, women's luxury designer fashions

LOCATION: 8300 Preston Rd.

Musical Venue Expands, But Remains True to Its Roots

House of Blues has expanded from its roots when it started as a tribute to blues, rhythm, gospel, jazz, and rock 'n' roll. The Dallas HOB is located at 2200 N. Lamar in a post-World War I era building north of Woodall Rogers and east of IH-35E. For years the three-story brick building served as a warehouse to White Swan Coffee Processing. The building was called "an excellent example of an early 20th century industrial facility" before being purchased in 2006 and extensively remodeled by Victory Park developer Hillwood Capital into the HOB.

On any given night, you can hear acts such as Robin Trower, The Fray, or preteen sensation Kidz Bop. While the new styles of music and entertainment once foreign to HOB dominate the headlines and pack the 2,500-seat musical venue, they have kept one popular weekly program true to its Southern gospel base.

Each Sunday morning, HOB hosts their heart-stopping, foot-pounding "World Famous Brunch Even Raises the Roof," featuring local and regional gospel groups that sing both traditional and contemporary gospel songs. Before and during the performance, attendees can take advantage of the all-you-can eat breakfast buffet, which includes carving stations, desserts, and the HOB specialty: chicken and waffles. Some patrons are so inspired by the sound that they wave their napkins and jump on stage.

The brunch's mottos include "Praise the Lord and pass the biscuits" and "You've got to sing it to believe it."

While tickets to the headliner events vary, the gospel celebration and breakfast buffet is $45.

Above: The White Swan Building was built in 1925 as the Waples-Platter Coffee Roaster Building. In 1978, it was included on the National Register of Historic Places. (Swan Building IPTC Photo Metadata.)

Right: House of Blues grew out of founder Isaac Tigrett's love for the blues. Since the first HOB opened in 1992 in Cambridge, Massachusetts, it has dedicated itself to celebrating the history of Southern culture and African artistic contributions to music. (Photo by Harry Hall.)

THIS USED TO BE: White Swan Coffee Processing
NOW IT'S: House of Blues
LOCATION: 2200 N. Lamar

DART Preserves Monroe Shops

Dallas Area Rapid Transit (DART) purchased the crumbling red brick 275-foot-long Monroe Shops Building at 2111 S. Corinth St., near the Illinois Street Station, in 1991. It wasn't until 2009 that the remodeling project, titled TRACK 3, began turning it into a DART police station.

The renovation team faced several challenges. First, the existing structure was 35,000 square feet, and the plan called for 65,000 square feet. So, they created a building-within-a-building concept. That strategy helped make the most of the existing space while still maintaining the original shop's integrity. The roof was reinforced, and architectural fixtures were restored. Three floors of workspace, meeting rooms, and offices replaced wide service aisles. The $20 million renovated structure opened in 2011.

From 1901 until 1948, a small electric train called the "interurban railway" proved a popular way of traveling from Dallas to towns not on

The growing DART rail system needed an expansion of its security force, so a successful renovation of the historical treasure, Monroe Shops, was completed in 2011. (Photo by Renelibrary Creative Commons Share Alike 3.0 Unported Renelibrary given photo credit.)

traditional train stops, such as Waxahachie, Corsicana, and Waco. Monroe Shops served as the maintenance facility for the rail lines, which at its peak totaled about 200 miles. The main bay had three tracks running the length of the building. The bay also included an inspection pit area and machine shop with tools for working on axels. A 15-ton box crane spanned the bay and ran along 21 feet above the floor, moving vehicles and equipment where needed. The upper level included offices and a lecture hall. After Interurban shut down, Monroe Shops was owned by a paper mill, U-Haul outlet, and the city of Dallas.

The new facility consolidated many DART functions under a more efficient and environmentally friendly building. With the police in the more convenient location, they now have easy access to more than 90 miles of rail.

Costly safety upgrades and a major rail accident in 1948 doomed the Interurban.

THIS USED TO BE: Monroe Shops Building
NOW IT'S: DART Police Station
LOCATION: 2111 S. Corinth St.

The Ladies of Frogtown

Frogtown.

The name originated from the frogs that traveled up the Trinity River to the area just under what is now Woodall Rodgers Freeway, around Griffin and Broom Streets, at the northeast tip of West End and south of Uptown near the Perot Museum. However, in the early 20th century, Frogtown became a flashpoint for Dallas's two factions of stark moral and societal differences.

On one side, the rough-and-tumble cowboys felt the need to let off steam after working long hours in a physically demanding profession. They battled the strict moral code laid out by the growing numbers of churches that encouraged biblical teachings.

City officials attempted a compromise in Frogtown where, for a few years, prostitution was legal. Consolidating the activity, the thought went, kept most of the city free from "fallen women" and would help the police do their jobs. Opponents claimed that since the public and law accepted the practice, their business would increase. By luck or design, one of the city's main streetcars ran right through Frogtown, and local girls could be seen on the streets, exhibiting virtually all their wares, prompting one visitor to comment they were, "practically unclothed, always eagerly, sometimes clamorously soliciting trade."

After years of battling, the pastors, women, and judges won out. Attorney General Currie McCutcheon announced on November 4, 1913, that the Frogtown brothels would close.

A handful of the newly unemployed women entered a sort of rehabilitation home; others reportedly moved to cities friendlier to their presence. Many said the crackdown would ruin their lives, as they needed the lucrative job to care for their children and mothers.

J.T. Upchurch published *The Purity Journal*, which gave Christians directions on how to reach out to the "fallen men and women" as well as the city's "street children."

Frogtown included what is now Woodall Rodgers Freeway and McKinney, not far from where Hooters stands today. While the area was designated for prostitutes to conduct business, no bars were allowed in the area. (From https://davidkirkpatrick.worldprss.com/tag/red-light-district.)

THIS USED TO BE: Frogtown, a place for legalized prostitution

NOW IT'S: Woodall Rodgers Freeway

LOCATION: NE tip of West End and south of Uptown, near Hooters

Woodruff Robbed of Record?

Following the success of the 1936 Centennial Texas State Fair, the Cotton Bowl, already football home to the SMU Mustangs and the Cotton Bowl Classic, played host to the first-ever Exposition Games. The games lasted 142 days from mid-June through late October 1937, and they showcased multiracial athletes from all over the Americas, including soccer, boxing and, of course, track and field, for which a temporary track was set up in the stadium.

The Exposition Games's 880-yard race was listed as a major highlight, maybe even the headliner. The contest featured 1936 Olympic Champion John Woodruff and Elroy Robinson, the latter fresh off his world-record performance in New York. Instead, it is remembered for being a moment of controversy that left Woodruff frustrated and angry about having a potentially stolen record, maybe because of his skin color.

Woodruff won the race in 1 minute, 47.8 seconds, easily besting Robinson and his world record of 1 minute, 49.6 seconds, but a post-racetrack remeasurement showed the track to be six feet short. Since the track was only temporary, nothing can be proven.

In an interview found on the National Visionary Leadership Project, Woodruff was quoted as saying, "You know what happened. Those boys got together and decided they weren't going to give a Black man a white man's record."

Despite the setback, Woodruff continued running on a national level, and in 1940, he set the 800-meter (metric equivalent of the 880) American record of 1 minute, 48.5 seconds.

Woodruff died in 2007 at age 92 without ever getting credit for his record-setting run in Dallas.

The Exposition Games led to the Pan-Am Games, a multisport competition held every four years for any country in the Americas.

Dallas's 1937 Greater Texas & Pan-American Exposition Games flopped and is largely forgotten. But the event set the stage for the Pan-American Games, which is held every four years in the year before the Olympic Games. (Postcard from 1937 Dallas Exposition Games.)

THIS USED TO BE: Home of the Exposition Games

NOW IT'S: Home of major college football games, concerts, and other events

LOCATION: 3750 Midway Plaza

Dallas Moves the Trinity River

The disastrous 1908 Trinity River flood resulted in the building of the Houston Street Viaduct, which would keep traffic flowing between Dallas and Oak Cliff over a swollen Trinity River. However, the bridge wouldn't prevent future flooding. The Trinity had flooded several times, but this time, the flood left 4,000 people homeless and did property damage of up to $5 million ($136 million in 2019 dollars). City officials agreed to an ambitious project: move the river.

In 1911, Dallas called St. Louis architect George Kessler to develop a system for flood control. After World War I and other delays, in 1925, the city-appointed Ulrickson Committee studied the 550-mile river and the 18,000 square miles that it drains. The committee recommended a Trinity Levee District to reclaim more than 10,500 acres of land by confining flooding to 4,000 acres between levees. It would include creating sewers, waterworks, and beautification. The levees would have the capacity to carry two-and-one-half times the volume of the 1908 Trinity River flood. Interior drainage would include seven gravity-flow sluiceways, four pumping plants, and five pressure sewer lines. The project would be paid for with a $23.9 million bond package, which was approved by December 1927. Other monies were donated or raised for additional upgrades.

Dredging began on July 24, 1928. It included the relocation of utilities, streetcars, telegraph poles, and oil, gas, water, and sewer lines. They moved 22 million cubic yards of dirt to relocate the river one half-mile west into the middle of the flood plain and built up the levees. On an average day, 1,000 men worked on the project. The Great Depression again delayed its completion, but it was finally done in 1932.

Dallas has flooded many times in the last 100 years, but nothing has compared to the devastation of the tragedy of 1908.

Using the Old Red Courthouse as a landmark on both maps, it's easy to see how much the Trinity River was moved. Today, it runs east to west, just south of Trinity Groves. (Pre-move: courtesy of SMU Libraries, Edwin J. Foscue Library, taken by Lloyd M. Long. Post-move: courtesy of Google Maps.)

Leslie Stemmons, who served on the Ulrickson Committee, learned the value of moving dirt in 1910 after watching the creation of the Panama Canal.

THIS USED TO BE: A flood-prone Trinity River

NOW IT'S: A rechanneled Trinity River

LOCATION: Between Oak Cliff and downtown Dallas

Lucky Lindy's Reputation Nosedives

Just east of Central Expressway and north of Interstate 635, Skillman Avenue begins its nine-mile south-southwest path through some fine established neighborhoods, including laid-back Lakewood, before it dead-ends into Junius St. and Lipscomb Elementary School. Skillman is a significant road for many Dallasites, but for 14 years, it was called Lindbergh Drive, after the country's aerial hero, Charles Lindbergh.

On September 27, 1927, Dallas was the center of the aviation universe. Lindbergh, aka "Lucky Lindy," just four months after making history with a solo 33.5-hour flight across the Atlantic Ocean, landed his Ryan mono plane, *Spirit of St. Louis*, at Love Field. Dallas was one stop of a 92-city tour to promote aviation. Thousands stood in the rain to see him receive Dallas's first ticker-tape parade. The route went from E. Lover's Lane to Preston, west on Elm, and east to Main Street to the Adolphus Hotel, where 700 of the city's most influential leaders threw him a grand reception. The guest list included local politicians, military officers, and Texas Governor Dan Moody. The city named a street, just northwest of White Rock Lake between Mockingbird and Swiss Avenue, Lindbergh Drive. However, Lindbergh drew controversy during World War II as he publicly took a dim view of America's potential involvement in the war.

As spokesperson for the America First Committee, he made statements that appeared to support Germany against possible US intervention in the conflict. Other remarks were interpreted as anti-Semitic, which he denied, but he took multiple trips to Germany, further damaging his reputation.

In response, the Dallas City Council voted to change every Lindbergh Drive sign to Skillman Street, named after local banker W. F. Skillman. The changes were made on December 5, 1941, just two days before the Japanese bombed Pearl Harbor, which forced the United States into World War II.

On September 27, 1927, Dallas gave aviator hero Charles Lindbergh its first ticker-tape parade. The city hosted a dinner at the Adolphus Hotel in his honor, an event with a guest list that included Texas Governor Dan Moody. However, Lindbergh's perceived controversial comments about Jews and American involvement in WWII damaged his reputation. (Dallas Public Library Frank Rogers Collection.)

Charles Lindbergh was *Time Magazine's* first, and still the youngest, "Man of the Year." Lindbergh received two medals from President Coolidge and had a stamp issued in his honor.

THIS USED TO BE: Lindbergh Dr.

NOW IT'S: Skillman St.

LOCATION: Northwest of White Rock Lake, between Mockingbird Ln. and Swiss Ave.

Dallas's Last Vaudeville House

The sign for the Majestic Theatre is, well, majestic. Running vertically the length of the 20th-century interpretation of the Renaissance Revival-style building, its red and white colors can be seen far from its home at 1925 Elm St. The sign is actually an arrow that points to a lighted awning just above the theater's entryways, with marquees announcing the theater's latest live attraction.

The Majestic opened on April 11, 1921, as the flagship project for the Interstate Amusement Company, which operated a chain of vaudeville houses. Bob Hope, Mary Pickford ("America's Sweetheart"), and even Harry Houdini appeared here. As vaudeville died out, the Majestic's offerings switched to movies, and in 1932, it became known as the "man's house," favoring the film noir of Warner Brothers stars Humphrey Bogart and James Cagney. (The nearby Palace House had the same format for women.)

On July 16, 1973, after a final showing of the James Bond film *Live and Let Die*, the Majestic Theatre, once the pride of theater row, closed.

In January 1976, the Hoblitzelle Foundation, which had established theaters throughout Texas and the southwest under the Interstate Theatre Company, turned the Majestic Theatre over to the city, which restored the venue, including the original Corinthian columns, balustrades, urns, and trellises. The orchestra pit was enlarged, necessitating a reduction in seating from 2,400 to 1,570. The balcony was rewired for electricity and sound. The stage was stabilized, and the wings were expanded. It reopened on January 28, 1983, and was the first Dallas Building to be listed in the National Register of Historic Places.

Although closed at the time, the Majestic was used for the concert scenes in Brian De Palma's 1974 film *Phantom of the Paradise*.

In the mid-1950s, fans lined up in front of the Majestic Theatre to watch the epic movie *Giant*. Note the Melba next door. These days, the Majestic is a performing arts center, and it was the first Dallas structure to be listed in the National Register of Historic Places. (Photo by WesODonnell. Creative Commons BY-SA 3.0)

THIS USED TO BE: Majestic Theatre, home of vaudeville acts and, later, movies

NOW IT'S: Majestic Theatre for performing arts

LOCATION: 1925 Elm St.

Cumberland School Makes Huge Transformation

Just south of Woodall Rogers Freeway, at 1901 Akard Street, near the new Fairmont Hotel, stands the mustard-colored, Victorian-style Cumberland Hill Building, converted from one of the oldest remaining schools in Dallas. When the school closed in 1969, the Dallas School Board put it up for sale. Just before meeting its doom, the Sedco Oil Company bought the school for $1.3 million. The company then put another $1 million for a near full restoration that included a new air-conditioning system for the 44,000 square feet of office space.

The transformation was not the school's first. The original wooden school was destroyed and then rebuilt in 1888 as one of the city's first brick schoolhouses, serving some of the Dallas elite and descendants of city founders. Residents of Ross, Thomas, McKinney, and Maple Avenues sent their children to this prestigious school. Reports are that some girls arrived daily in stylish carriages driven by liveried coachmen.

By the 1930s, industry moved in, displacing many of the neighborhood families and giving the school one of the city's most diverse populations. In 1955, a fire at nearby Travis Elementary necessitated displaced students to transfer to Cumberland Hill. It became the main school for Little Mexico, as about 90% of the students were then Hispanic. One former student said they had three children for each textbook; a television report stated that many students didn't attend school because their parents lacked transportation. Travis was rebuilt, and Cumberland enrollment kept declining. In 1963, it operated as a publicly funded trade school, supplying skilled specialists necessary to help create industrial and business expansion.

Today, the Cumberland Hill School Building is home to 23 companies, including oil and gas exploration and investment outfits.

Cumberland Hill started out as a school for Dallas elites, but by the 1930s it counted 25 nationalities in its student body. Industrialization soon grew around it, necessitating its closing in 1969. Now refurbished, it is home to nearly two dozen companies. (Photo by Harry Hall.)

One of the school's first students was Jesse Jones, Secretary of Commerce during World War II.

THIS USED TO BE: Cumberland Hill School

NOW IT'S: Cumberland Hill School Building, office space

LOCATION: 1901 Akard St.

Interurban Rail Creates Progress in Transportation

Within an easy walk to many restaurants, the J. Erik Jonsson Central Library, and the Belo Garden, the eight-story, red brick, classical revival Interurban Building has a lot of appeal. In addition to its 134 lofts, it features covered and guarded parking. It is part of a fascinating and important part of Dallas's growth.

In the early 20th century, much of Dallas was dirt roads while the city transitioned from horse to mechanical, steam, and electrical transportation. The lack of reliable routes made travel difficult for wheeled vehicles. The interurban (or radial railway) was the answer. Smaller than locomotives, the electric-driven interurban railways made efficient transportation possible between underserved communities, delivering people, mail, and freight to stops bypassed by bigger trains.

Interurban started in 1901, when the Denison & Sherman Railway Company laid 10 miles of track between those two cities. Over the next few years, through a series of other company purchases and takeovers, more than 200 miles of interurban track was laid, extending the train to Waco. In 1916, the $1.5 million Interurban Train Station was built at what is now 1500 Jackson Street to accommodate the 35 trains that drove the routes. But roads improved, and cars became more affordable and attractive, and through the 1930s and 1940s, the need for the interurban diminished. The interurban died out on December 31, 1948, and few remnants remain.

In the 1950s, the Interurban Building Train Station became home for the Trailways Bus Company until they were bought by Greyhound in 1987, when the building was vacated. In January 2019, the property was bought by AT&T, which had no immediate plans to make dramatic changes to the lofts.

This apartment building was once the main station to the electricity-powered interurban rail lines. The cars were popular and would carry people and even packages to towns bypassed by the major trains, such as Corsicana, Waco, and Waxahachie. (Interurban Railway public domain, author: Brandon Cooper. https://creativecommons.org/licenses/by/2.0/deed.en.)

Plano is home to the Interurban Railway Museum, where a restored Texas Electric Railway car is on display.

THIS USED TO BE: Interurban Building Train Station
NOW IT'S: Interurban Building Apartments
LOCATION: 1500 Jackson St.

The Colorful Legacy of the Longhorn Ballroom

"When it comes to history and intrigue, no Texas dance hall can match the Dallas club built for Bob Wills," said Coy Prather at *Texas Music Magazine*.

The Longhorn Ballroom lives up to its name. Its recently upgraded restaurant now hosts several events, including weddings, dance classes, and even horseback-riding lessons.

The marquee and 1,000-seat ballroom are shaped like a barn, but the most obvious clue is the giant longhorn statue out front. The ballroom is located just south of the Cedars area, at Corinth and Riverfront, and features a fence and gated area that has the look of a wagon wheel, with a giant star in the middle.

When speaking of the Longhorn Ballroom, it's difficult to say which is more colorful: the management or the acts. The club originated in 1950, when eccentric Dallas millionaire O. L. Nelms named his new musical venue Bob Wills's Ranch House, after his close friend Bob Wills, "The King of Western Swing." Nelms leased the club to Jack Ruby, who would later kill President Kennedy's assassin, Lee Harvey Oswald. In 1978, Nelms sold the club to Danny Groom, who not only gave the venue its current name, but elevated its status into a top country and western theme, with western memorabilia, a barbeque restaurant and, most notably, a 21-foot-long longhorn statue with 18-inch horns.

Over the years, stage acts included Nat King Cole, BB King, the Red Hot Chili Peppers, and Loretta Lynn. The ballroom once scheduled punk rockers the Sex Pistols one night and country legend Merle Haggard the next.

After changing ownership over the years, in 2017, the club was bought by Jay LaFrance, who appreciated the club's historic significance and upgraded it to more than a bar.

The club made international news when a woman head-butted the Sex Pistols's Sid Vicious after he taunted the crowd of 800.

Millionaire O. L. Nelms built the dance club for his friend Bob Wills, often called, "The King of Western Swing." The Bob Wills Ranch House saw country performers such as Charley Pride, Ray Price, and Loretta Lynn. Today, as the Longhorn Ballroom, it hosts a variety of events, from weddings to horseback riding. Note the longhorn under the sign. (Photo by Harry Hall.)

Postcard of the Bob Wills's Ranch House. (Boston Public Library, digitalcommonwealth.org.)

THIS USED TO BE: Bob Wills's Ranch House
NOW IT'S: The Longhorn Ballroom
LOCATION: 216 Corinth St.

Dying 110-Year-Old School Gets New Life

In 2016, developer Matthews Southwest bought the abandoned Dallas High School on Bryan St. and began a $50 million renovation plan that would turn the building into a 100,000-square-foot mixed-use development structure. Approximately two-thirds of the building would be office space and the remaining one-third retail. The developers used virtually everything in the building that wasn't damaged from age and deterioration.

Since its closure in 1995, Dallas High School, built in 1907, seemed ready for the wrecking ball. The three-and-a-half-story classical revival structure stood as one of Dallas's oldest buildings but sat empty for nearly 20 years. It was placed on preservationists' most endangered list, and four of the five buildings that originally made up the school had been destroyed. The remaining structure, the main building, survived only through the efforts of a city ordinance, Dallas historians, preservationists, and alumni. It eventually became a city landmark, which meant that any restoration would require keeping the exterior intact.

Over the decades, the school was known by many names: N. R. Crozier Technical High School, Main High School, and Bryan High School. In the 1940s, under the name Crozier Tech, it became the Dallas School District's business magnet school. Like modern magnet schools, students from throughout the district were invited to attend, and many did. Crozier Tech offered four "general divisions of study" and classes in automotive repair, woodworking, architectural drawing, and stenography. Students also produced knives for the troops. It's said that at least 1,000 knives were made bearing a "Tech High" engraving on the blade.

Before the renovation was completed, over half the building had been leased. The largest lessee was the architectural firm Perkins & Will, which secured almost 40,000 square feet.

The main entrance leads straight to the Pearl/Arts District DART rail station.

In 2004, Preservation Texas added Dallas High School (aka Crozier Tech) to its inaugural list of "Texas's Most Endangered Historic Places." Many alums stepped in to save the building, and today, after a $50 million renovation by Matthews Southwest, it is a mixed-use development. (https://creativecommons.org/licenses/by-sa/4.0/deed.en.)

THIS USED TO BE: Dallas High School

NOW IT'S: Multi-use office and retail space

LOCATION: 2218 Bryan St.

Will Millennials Hang Out at This Former A-List Hotel?

The Cabana Motor Hotel was once owned by Doris Day, and its creation overseen by Jimmy Hoffa. Raquel Welch once worked there as a waitress. Guests included Led Zeppelin, Jimi Hendrix, and The Beatles.

The 10-story modern-design motor hotel opened in 1963 at 899 Stemmons Frwy. (across from what is now Victory Plaza) at a cost of $6 million. It was a development of Jay Sarno, who also built Caesar's Palace in Las Vegas. It had 300 rooms, 57 of them suites, and amenities that included a pool, spa, health club, restaurants, night clubs, and a ballroom. A Roman theme was carried throughout the interior, with columns and Roman-style figures woven into the carpet. The waitresses wore short, lacy togas with touches of gold and were called goddesses. Although popular with the Hollywood A-list crowd, by the late 1960s, the hotel

fell into hard times. In 1969, it was sold to Hyatt and renamed the Hyatt House Hotel, and then DuPont Plaza. In 1984, the county bought it for $9.2 million and until 2013, it served as a minimum-security jail.

Except for the bulldozers, road movers, and heavy trucks, the parking lot for the one-time Cabana Motor Hotel remains empty. Even the Cabana sign is gone. The roads leading to the hotel are closed, and a link fence circles the building. After years of abandonment, the Cabana is

Doris Day was reportedly furious that her husband, Martin Melcher, invested so much of her money into the Cabana.

The Cabana has a rich history, having been associated with Doris Day, Jimmy Hoffa, and Raquel Welch. Guests have included Led Zeppelin and Jimi Hendrix. The Beatles stayed here during their only Dallas visit in 1964. Now it's being renovated as a club and restaurant. (Photo on previous page by Harry Hall. Vintage Postcard October 12, 1967: [Cabaña Motor Hotel], postcard, 1967; https://texashistory.unt.edu/ark:/67531/metapth121563/: accessed September 1, 2019; University of North Texas Libraries, The Portal to Texas History, https://texashistory.unt.edu; crediting Dallas Heritage Village.)

undergoing renovation by Centurion American, the same company that bought and refurbished the Statler Hilton. Purchasing the Cabana cost the company $8.1 million, which many considered a steal for a motor hotel with such a rich Dallas history.

Mehrdad Moayedi, who runs Centurion American, plans on keeping the structure a hotel and a place where millennials can hang out, with a nightclub and a couple of restaurants.

THIS USED TO BE: Cabana Motor Hotel
NOW IT'S: A renovation project
LOCATION: 899 Stemmons Frwy.

The Lakewood Theater Is Spared

The notice in the window of the abandoned Lakewood Theater told locals something was up. It stated that an application to sell and consume alcohol had been filed with the city of Dallas, and that applicant was Bowlski's Lakewood, LLC. The new owners were Craig and Jennifer Spivey, longtime Lakewood residents and avid bowlers. The couple, having opened a Bowlski's in Colorado and Bowlounge in Dallas, wanted to bring their renovation skills to the Lakewood and turn it into a bowling alley.

The Lakewood Theater opened in 1938 with Mickey Rooney and Judy Garland in *Love Finds Andy Hardy*. In addition to movies, it has hosted live shows and special events. Its stage showcased live acts such as Cyndi Lauper, Gavin DeGraw, Erasure, and even burlesque shows. But it was more than that. When a neighborhood church burned down, they held services in Lakewood's 1,100-seat movie house. It hosted Woodrow Wilson High School graduation ceremonies. Its success as Dallas's first $1 theater created a popular movie-marketing strategy. One popular event was *The Rocky Horror Picture Show*.

It's had low spots, closing twice and going through four owners, and faced challenges from multi-screen theaters with better locations, but it always remained a movie house. After its closing in 2015, it seemed destined to become a restaurant.

Then the Spiveys stepped in and began the transformation. While a significant renovation was critical, such as ripping out the seats and installing 10 lanes from an abandoned bowling alley in Mineola, Texas, the couple maintained much of what made Lakewood special, such as the murals, bathroom tiles, and piano-shaped ceiling mirror.

Jennifer Spivey's father performed on the Lakewood stage with longtime favorite local band The Nightcaps.

Although Lakewood's purpose has changed considerably, much of the interior is intact. The art deco-style artwork, the mirrors on the ceiling, and stair banisters are just some of the familiar décor that remains from the theater days. (Photo by Harry Hall.)

THIS USED TO BE: Lakewood Theater

NOW IT'S: Bowlski's

LOCATION: 1825 Abrams Pkwy. #1

When Dallas Put Trains Underground

A metal door in the covered parking lot of the Garment Center Santa Fe Building hides what was once a lifeline for a city that struggled to keep up with its rapid growth.

By the mid-1920s, Dallas had outgrown its transportation systems. Trains, streetcars, and the newly appeared automobiles were making pedestrian life difficult and dangerous. The city came up with a novel idea to at least partially remedy the problem. They built an underground rail system, using four buildings as delivery and pick-up stops.

Employing the efforts of architect Lloyd Whitson, who worked with city officials, Dallas created an imaginative line that resulted in three sets of underground rails running north to south from Commerce to Young Streets. The tracks branched out from one line, centralizing the Gulf, Colorado, and Santa Fe Railroads' transfer and warehouse operations.

The creation of the underground line became one of Dallas's most ambitious building projects, resulting in one of the region's largest merchandising centers. The four brick and terra-cotta buildings were visually tied together by their common use of materials, reflecting the simplifying influences of modern architecture on large building construction. The 20-story Santa Fe Office Building, which faced Commerce Street and served as the train's headquarters, the Garment Center, and the Ingram Freezer Building, a refrigerated storage facility. The fourth building was a warehouse.

Thirty-five to 40 railcars ran through the tunnel daily, pulled by a "hot water bottle" locomotive, one of only two known to exist. It prevented smoke from accumulating in the tunnel.

About 1950, above-ground railcars and freight elevators replaced the need for the underground trains. Today, the Santa Fe Office Building houses space for federal government, and the garment center is now SoCo Urban Lofts. Both are listed in the National Register of Historic Places. The Ingram Freezer Building is a parking lot, and the warehouse is the Dallas Aloft Hotel.

Built in 1924, the Santa Fe Railroad Complex centralized the Gulf, Colorado, and Santa Fe Railroads in a network of rail tunnels that relieved congestion in downtown Dallas. Three of the four buildings remain, but the train tunnels were closed off to the public years ago. (Austrini; https://creativecommons.org/licenses/by/2.0/deed.en.)

During Prohibition, the railroad might have served a more insidious purpose: to run illegal alcohol into one of the buildings, specifically to building #2, since it was home to the University Club, an upscale men's facility that was added to the building's roof.

THIS USED TO BE: Santa Fe Underground Terminal Complex

NOW IT'S: Tunnel remnants, abandoned

LOCATION: Commerce to Young Streets

A Major Golf Tournament Got Its Start Here

Just about five miles northeast of downtown Dallas, southwest of White Rock Lake, stands the prestigious Country Club. Established in 1912, it remains one of the city's oldest private golf courses. Membership is by invitation only, and currently there is an extensive wait list. While the golf course is the star, it has other amenities, inluding the fitness center and spa, tennis court, Kidz Club, and youth activities such as cooking classes and movie nights. The course covers more than 6,700 yards and is a par 71. In 1944, the Lakewood hosted the PGA Texas Victory Open, in which Byron Nelson won by 10 strokes over his friend Harold "Jug" McSpaden. Ray Mangrum and Ben Hogan tied for third. For the victory, Nelson earned $2,667.67 in war bonds.

Over the next two years, the tournament changed names and locations, and Nelson went on to have one of the most impressive runs in golf history, winning 26 tournaments and a still-record 11 straight. But the Texas Victory Open and Nelson's streak set the stage for a PGA golf tournament in Dallas. For the next few years, the tournament was off and on before becoming an annual event. From 1956 to 1967, the contest was held at the Oak Cliff Country Club. Then in 1968, the tournament was moved to Preston Trail, and the name was changed to the Byron Nelson Golf Tournament. From 1983 to 2018, it was hosted by the Four Seasons at the Las Colinas Sports Club before it moved to the Trinity Forest Golf Club, southeast of downtown Dallas.

Although Lakewood is no longer on the PGA Tour, on June 24 and 25 it played host to the 2019 Club Care NTPGA Senior Professional Championship.

Since its official inception in 1968, The Nelson is the PGA Tour's most successful fundraiser, with $143 million.

When Byron Nelson won the 1944 Texas Victory Open, held at Lakewood, it set the stage for the Byron Nelson Golf Tournament, which annually raises funds for the Salesmanship Club of Dallas. (Vintage photo: DeGolyer Library, SMU; George W. Cook Texas Image Collection. Modern photo: Harry Hall.)

THIS USED TO BE: Home of the Texas Open
NOW IT'S: The Lakewood Country Club
LOCATION: 1912 Abrams Pkwy.

It Really Was a Bomb Factory, Sort of

After 18 years of neglect, the one-time automobile assembly plant at 2713 Canton in Deep Ellum was reopened as a musical venue known as The Bomb Factory. It hosted acts such as The Ramones, Black Sabbath, and Phish, but an economic downturn forced its closing again in 1997. In November 2013, Clint Barlow, owner of musical venue Trees Dallas, bought and renovated The Bomb Factory and reopened it in 2015.

The result was stunning. The beige brick industrial building was reconfigured to accommodate 4,300. The 50,000-square-foot arena facelift included upgraded air-conditioning, the addition of mezzanine seating, and VIP suites, all contributing to an enhanced concert-going experience. Since Barlow took over, Robert Plant, Hardwell, Sturgill Simpson, and Lauryn Hill have all performed there.

The Bomb Factory's history and source of its great name goes back more than 100 years.

In 1914, young automobile magnate Henry Ford bought the land at the block of 2700 Williams Street (now Canton) and across the street from the Adams Hat Factory. It was one of Ford's first assembly plants outside of Detroit, and it would remain so until World War II, when Ford was pressured into transforming his facility for the manufacturing of jeeps, ammunition, and practice bombs. It then operated under the name "Mayhew Machine and Engineering Works."

Facing an economic turndown, Mayhew's closed in the 1970s and remained dormant for about 15 years, when the revitalization of Deep Ellum included commercial development and as a place for jazz and blues created renewed interest in both the area and Mayhew's.

The Bomb Factory's sold-out 2015 grand opening was headlined by Dallas musicians Erykah Badu and Sarah Jaffe.

While today's Bomb Factory is a popular venue for musical events, at one time it was owned by Henry Ford. Under the name "Mayhew Machine and Engineering Works," it made all kinds of military equipment, including practice bombs. (Photo by Harry Hall.)

The Bomb Factory has grown its entertainment variety. In addition to music, on November 28, 2015, it hosted the NBC-televised Premier Boxing Champions Super Welterweight World Championship.

THIS USED TO BE: Mayhew Machine and Engineering Works

NOW IT'S: The Bomb Factory

LOCATION: 2713 Canton St.

Plans for Cedars Development Go Up in Smoke

Residents of the Cedars area of Dallas were looking forward to the change involving the Ambassador Hotel, the neighborhood's signature building. Jim Lake and his wife, Amanda Moreno, who had already infused life into a dying Bishop Arts District in Oak Cliff, purchased the abandoned Ambassador Hotel with big plans. They would turn it into 103 upper-class apartments, a revision that included a pool, retail space, working space, and a speakeasy. The plans literally went up in smoke at 1:30 a.m. on May 28, 2019, when for reasons still unknown, the 115-year old Ambassador Hotel went down in flames. Nearly 100 firefighters worked to put out the fire, which didn't spread to nearby structures. The damage was so extensive that the building was declared a total loss. No one was injured.

Originally called The Majestic when built in 1905, the Ambassador Hotel was the finest in Dallas. Sarah Bernhardt and other A-list celebrities stayed there during Dallas performances. Over the years, the hotel faced the same obstacles that have befallen many other long-standing establishments. It eventually became a retirement home, a Christian school, and a movie set. The building had been abandoned for several years when Lake and Moreno bought it.

The Ambassador Hotel could have brought new residents and new life to the fading Cedars area, but now the future is in doubt. At the remnants of the Ambassador stands a sign promising "Development underway by Jim Lake."

Three US presidents—Theodore Roosevelt, William Taft, and Woodrow Wilson—have spent the night in the Ambassador Hotel.

Headed for a major upgrade, the Ambassador Hotel, where three US presidents stayed, went up in flames on May 28, 2019. The cause is unknown, but it was a total loss. The oldest hotel in Dallas was selected as a Texas Historic Landmark in 1965 and named as a city historic landmark in 1982. (Photo by Renelibrary. https://creativecommons.org/licenses/by-sa/4.0/deed.en.)

THIS USED TO BE: The Ambassador Hotel

NOW IT'S: Destroyed

LOCATION: 1312 S. Ervay St.

The First International Hotel Chain Started in Dallas

The Hotel Indigo is what you'd expect in a prestigious downtown hotel. It even looks the part. Standing 14 stories at the corner of Main and S. Harwood Streets, it's a Sullivan style with a horseshoe design, symmetrical facades, and Beaux Arts detailing. A $5 million renovation added hardwood floors, upgraded bathrooms, and larger guest rooms. That was just the latest upgrade for a hotel that started the trend in 1925 as the first hotel to bear the name "Hilton."

Unlike earlier hotels started by Conrad Hilton, which were renovation projects, he designed this one from top to bottom. Hilton maximized all available space in the public areas of the hotel for an assortment of customer convenience, including a druggist, men's shop, barbershop, valet service, beauty shop, and coffee shop. Hilton said that the rent on those stores supplemented the finances of the operation. The 325 guest rooms were painted in pearl gray or cream. They were small, but each one was carpeted and had a full or half-bath. In those pre-air-conditioning days, avoiding western-facing windows was critical in keeping the room temperature tolerable against the brutal Dallas summer heat, so 75% of the rooms had either southern or eastern exposure.

In subsequent years, the hotel underwent several ownership and name changes. The building continued a steady decline throughout the 1970s. In 2006, InterContinental Hotels Group, parent company of Holiday Inn, converted the hotel to Hotel Indigo Dallas Downtown.

Conrad Hilton's 1984 book, *Be My Guest*, is still considered a must-read for hoteliers.

Originally the Dallas Hilton, it was the first structure Conrad Hilton designed from the ground up. Hilton got into the hotel business after seeing a line at the Cisco, Texas, Mobley Hotel where he was staying. The owner, ready to retire, dismissed expanding, so Hilton bought the hotel and began upgrades. (https://creativecommons.org/licenses/by-sa/3.0/deed.en. Attribution: MIB at English Wikipedia.)

THIS USED TO BE: Hilton Hotel

NOW IT'S: Hotel Indigo

LOCATION: 1933 Main St.

The French-Influenced Wilson Building

The city of Dallas bought the eight-story Wilson Building in 1999 for $3.4 million. It was then leased and turned into 135 apartments and penthouses, featuring hardwood floors, a theater room, on-site restaurants, and a rooftop deck, thus creating the Wilson Apartments.

Patterned after the Palais Garnier in Paris, France, the E-shaped structure with rounded corners occupies the east half of the block bounded by Main, Ervay, Elm, and Stone streets. The Wilson has seen massive internal upgrades, perhaps most notably air-conditioning in 1949, but the inside features marble floors, wainscoting, and world-class mahogany doors and window casings.

The outside has been called "a modern adaptation of French Renaissance," and it looks the same as when built in 1904 with glazed brick, enameled terra-cotta columns, and carved and decorated marble arch.

In 1872, Canadian-born J. B. Wilson left Louisiana, where he'd been the boss of a logging camp, and came to Dallas about the same time as the railroad. Wilson made his first success in cattle, then banking and investing. But his greatest achievement might have been in architecture, where he designed what was then the tallest and grandest building in Dallas. His legacy is carried on in his creation, as the metal on all light switches and many other original fixtures are marked with the initials J.B.W.

Originally, the basement and first two floors were part of the Titche-Goettinger Company, with whom Wilson had a financial interest. Upper floors were office space. Over the next several decades, W. A. Green Department Store and H. L. Green Variety Store later moved in. The latter moved out in 1997, just two years before Dallas purchased it.

In October 1961, the Wilson Building, then the home of H. L. Green Variety Store, became the first in downtown Dallas to desegregate its lunch counter. (https://creativecommons.org/licenses/by/3.0/deed.en. Author: Dfwcre8tive.)

THIS USED TO BE: The Wilson Building

NOW IT'S: The Wilson Apartments

LOCATION: 1623 Main St.

Dallas World Aquarium: More Than Fish

The sign announcing "The Dallas World Aquarium" is mounted across the building's top story—a greenhouse-looking tower easily seen just south of Woodall Rogers Freeway near its junction of Interstate 35—on the outskirts of Dallas's historic West End.

The building exhibits a postmodern architectural style, with a rather wild and asymmetrical design. Since opening in 1992, the aquarium has become so popular that it has expanded twice. The main section, a warehouse built in 1924, was home to several industries, including a rubber company and a steel-and-die outfit. The first expansion replaced a one-time venetian blind company that later became a Hispanic-themed restaurant and bar. The final addition occurred in 2000 with the purchase of a vacant lot.

Visitors will hear several Dallas World Aquarium greetings even before beginning the long, winding concrete walkway that leads uphill to the official entrance. With exotic plants, fish in simulated natural habitats and traditional aquariums, and screeching and squawking from birds on either side, one immediately realizes that this is more than a home for aquatic life. It's more of a combination zoo-aquarium.

Manatees, more birds, alligators, monkeys, reptiles, and all types of mammals highlight what has become a major attraction to both Dallas residents and tourists. Crowd-favorite attractions include the shark tunnels, several species of seahorses, and a toucan whom patrons can feed (provided he is hungry).

Each October 17, the aquarium joins several organizations in celebrating International Sawfish Day, which raises awareness of this endangered fish.

In addition to sea life, the aquarium is home to birds, sloths, crocodiles, and a reproduction of a rain forest. (Photo by Jay R. Simonson. https://creativecommons.org/licenses/by-sa/3.0/deed.en.)

THIS USED TO BE: Warehouses and a parking lot

NOW IT'S: Dallas World Aquarium

LOCATION: 1801 North Griffin St.

Accredited by the Association of Zoos and Aquariums (1997) and member of the World Association of Zoos and Aquariums (since 2000).

HOURS: 9 a.m. to 5 p.m. daily. Tickets range from $14.95 to $20.95, with discounts for seniors. Admission for children under two is free.

Don't Mess with My Tex-Mex

In 2008, when Firebird Restaurant Group bought 22 El Fenix Restaurants for $30 million from the founding Martinez family, they promised not to mess with the recipes that had become so popular in the restaurant's 90 years. They made preparation adjustments, called "tweaking," to help speed the cooking. However, the devoted clientele let management know of their disapproval, and Firebird quickly retreated to the original recipe.

Located in what was then called Little Mexico, an area that was displaced with the construction of Woodall Rogers Freeway in 1965, the original El Fenix moved across the street from 1608 to 1601 McKinney Ave. The Spanish-style restaurant has a hacienda-like atmosphere both inside and out. The red and turquoise neon sign not only announces the establishment's name but also proclaims its existence "Since 1918," making it the oldest Tex-Mex restaurant chain in America.

The current El Fenix is across the street from its original location. It moved in 1965. (Photo by Jamey Key.)

After the move, the eatery started what would become the franchise's signature dining special. Each Wednesday, El Fenix sponsors a $5.99 special: two hand-rolled cheese, chicken, or beef enchiladas with rice and beans. According to Alfred Martinez, son of founder Mike, the downtown location serves 1,200 Wednesday lunches and the same number at dinner.

El Fenix was founded in 1918 by Mike Martinez, who had previously worked as a cook for Dallas's Oriental Hotel. His original menu included oysters and spaghetti in addition to what would famously become Tex-Mex, introducing entrees such as enchiladas, frijoles, and chili con carne.

What separates El Fenix from many other restaurants is the devotion

Miguel Martinez, a dishwasher at Dallas's Oriental Hotel, opened the Martinez Café in his house. He started serving American food, but quickly changed the name to El Fenix, with a menu that combined American with Mexican favorites, thus inventing Tex-Mex. Today, the franchise has grown to 22 locations. (Photo from 1940 postcard. Elfenix.com.)

of its clientele. Senior VP of Operations Tim Schroder estimates that about 20% of their customers have been eating at El Fenix for more than 50 years. El Fenix has won *D Magazine* Reader's Choice Awards for "Best Tex-Mex" and has been a multiple winner of DFW's "Best Margarita."

In 2015, then-Dallas Mayor Mike Rawlings saved a customer from choking by using the Heimlich maneuver; now Rawlings has an El Fenix holiday named after him.

THIS USED TO BE: A parking lot
NOW IT'S: El Fenix Restaurant
LOCATION: 1608 McKinney Ave.

Not the Cowboys' "Field of Dreams"

Standing in the southwest Dallas field enclosed by East Jefferson Boulevard to the west, Brazos Street to the north, Colorado Boulevard to the south, and the Trinity River to the east provides a marvelous view of downtown and Dallas's two new signature bridges—Margaret Hunt Ill and Margaret McDermott. The empty ground belies its significance. From 1924 to 1964, this plot was home to several minor-league baseball teams, most notably the Eagles, who called Burnett Field home from 1948 to 1958. Both Joe DiMaggio and Willie Mays played in exhibition games there.

In 1960, the 10,500-seat ballpark served as home to the Dallas Cowboys' first training camp. Gil Brandt, the Dallas Cowboys' original vice president of player personnel, said in an August 2016 *Dallas Morning News* Sports Day interview that in 1960, the NFL's newest franchise had a simple reason for using Burnett Field: "It was available."

"Burnett Field was terrible, rat infested. Guys had to hang their jerseys on pipes so the rats didn't eat them," said Brandt, now an NFL Hall of Famer. The training room doubled as the women's restroom. It got so cold in the winter that one player, near the end of the team's winless first season, built a fire by his locker.

In 1963, the Cowboys moved to an established facility on North Central Expressway and Yale Boulevard when the previous tenant, the AFL's Dallas Texans, moved to Kansas City and became the Chiefs. In 1964, after 40 years of serving as home to several minor-league baseball teams, the most recent being the Dallas Eagles, Burnett Field closed.

The Eagles became the Dallas-Fort Worth Spurs, joined the Texas League, and moved to Turnpike Stadium in Arlington. Burnett Field was torn down in 1966 and has since remained a grassy plot of land.

Good Ol' Dave's Pawn Shop bought an outfield ad featuring a shotgun. If a player hit the shotgun, he won it.

Yankee greats Joe DiMaggio (left) and Gil McDougald (right) pose for a shot at Burnett Field, probably in the spring of 1951. (Photo: Joe DiMaggio and Gil McDougald at Burnett Field Dallas Public Library Historic Photograph collection. From the Hayes collection.)

From the 1940s to the 1960s, Burnett Field was home to Dallas minor-league baseball and major-league exhibition games. In 1960, it served as the practice facility for the Dallas Cowboys. The minor-league teams moved out, and the field came down in 1964. (Burnett Field Wikimapia.)

THIS USED TO BE: Burnett Field

NOW IT'S: Grassland

LOCATION: 1500 E. Jefferson Blvd.

The Little Oak Cliff Store That Grew to Worldwide Prominence

The small, white building with the turquoise overhang and a virtually all-window front doesn't attract a lot of attention from passersby. There's no corner sign and no marquee or flashing lights to point out its function. The only indication of its purpose is an almost insignificant-looking note marked just above the structure's door and 345 address: "LULAC National Educational Services, Inc." The LULAC (League of United Latin American Citizens) Education Service Center assists Hispanics with education, social, and legal issues. The building's history goes back more than a century for those in this quiet Oak Cliff neighborhood. The organization represented the start of an international corporation that would in many ways become the face of Dallas.

In 1910, eight-year-old Oak Cliff resident Joe C. "Jodie" Thompson cleaned stalls and fed the animals owned by Oak Cliff-based Consumer Ice Company. He moved up to loading ice on company trucks before graduating from the University of Texas with a business degree.

In 1927, Thompson negotiated a Southland Ice buyout of Consumer Ice, a deal that included making himself director. At the behest of his customers, Thompson began selling milk, bread, and cigarettes out of a small-frame store with a wooden awning and front porch at the corner of 12th Street and Edgefield Avenue. The expanded product line helped with sales during the slower winter months. He bought totem poles from Alaska and displayed them in front of the store as a marketing gimmick, calling his new enterprise "Tote'm Store."

By 1936, Tote'm was the area's largest carrier of dairy products, and the company started Oak Farm Dairies. After World War II, the advertising agency Tracy-Locke, capitalizing on the company's expanded store hours, changed the name to 7-Eleven. Today, 7-Eleven has more than 60,000 stores worldwide, and most are now open 24 hours a day. And the company still calls Dallas home.

The world's first convenience store was at 345 S. Edgefield (at 12th St). It started delivering ice, then cold watermelon (a true delight in Dallas summers), then milk and eggs, until 7-Eleven grew to an international corporation. (Photo from *Oh Thank Heaven! The Story of the Southland Corporation*, published by the Southland Corporation; author Allen Liles.)

The building was converted from a later 7-Eleven and is home to LULAC Education Centers, whose goal is to increase educational opportunities for Hispanic Americans. (Photo by Harry Hall.)

The Thompson family still owns about five percent of Southland Corporation.

THIS USED TO BE: The world's first convenience store

NOW IT'S: LULAC National Educational Service Centers

LOCATION: 345 South Edgefield Ave.

Women's Center Honors One of Dallas's Great Ones

Except for one lavender-painted wall that broadcasts the name, The WiNGS (Women in Need of Generous Support) Center Ebby's Place is a bland, beige building that covers the Modern Architecture design of the two-story building at 2603 Inwood Road, not far from the Medical District and Love Field. It has a gated, secured parking lot with security cameras. View blockers add to visitor and employee privacy.

The WiNGS Center Ebby's Place annually serves 3,000 needy women and children. It offers several life-centric programs, including financial literacy, childbirth education, parenting, nutrition, and wellness. Professional-themed classes teach entrepreneurship, resume writing, job searching and interviewing, and computer skills.

In the past, the 52-year-old structure has been home to the YWCA and, most recently, the American Medical Response and Emergency Medical Services. In 2015, a local nonprofit organization took it over and, after a $7 million renovation, created a facility that has given a huge boost to Dallas's underserved who are battling poverty. In the process, they honored a Dallas legend.

Ebby's Place was named for Ebby Halliday, in celebration of her 103rd birthday. Halliday, who died six months later, was a longtime real estate entrepreneur who had become one of the city's most recognizable citizens, and a beloved and admired figure throughout the world.

Ebby's Place offers free Wi-Fi, and children are welcome to attend any program.

According to YWCA CEO Jennifer Ware, "Here in Dallas County, one in three single female-led households lives below the poverty line."

This WiNGS facility serves about 3,000 needy moms annually, providing them with life skills such as resume writing, computer education, and personal finances. Those eligible include any first-time mother living in Dallas County who is less than 28 weeks pregnant and who qualifies for WIC or Medicaid services. (Courtesy of Harry Hall.)

THIS USED TO BE: American Medical Response Building

NOW IT'S: The WiNGS Center at Ebby's Place

LOCATION: 2603 Inwood Rd.

Inn of the Dove Was a Godsend for Blacks

The Inn of the Dove looks much like its early post-World War II years. Each of the 30 red-brick buildings has white vertical and horizontal posts in front. The units form a wide C, giving each guest an opportunity to drive their car into the private garage adjacent to each room. Amenities that once included a swimming pool, coffee shop, and soda fountain are gone. The Inn of the Dove was damaged by fire, and sometime in the early 1950s, owner Cora Reynolds was convicted of using the motel as a brothel.

Dove has survived under a string of names: Triple "R", Triple "A" and Ranch Motel, and it is one of many budget motels on Ft. Worth Avenue near where it crosses Interstate 30: Motel 6, Comfort, Shady Oaks, Palomino. But Dove differs in at least one respect. For six years, it was included in the recently rediscovered *Green Book*, meaning it was one of a handful of motels in the metroplex that catered to Black patrons.

The Inn of the Dove looks very much like it has for years. The private garages are a nice touch for guests. (Photo by Harry Hall.)

Throughout the Jim Crow era (1936–1966), *The Negro Motorist Green Book*, conceived by New York City mailman Victor Hugo Green, provided listings for businesses that were friendly to Blacks. Included were entries for hotels, service stations, garages, restaurants, and others. It became "the bible of Black travel during Jim Crow." Locally, most were near North Hall Street and Ross Avenue, near Freedman's settlement and Fair Park.

The only other known *Green Book* building still standing is the downtown Moorland YMCA, now home to the Black Dance Theater.

```
Corsicana
    Mrs. R. Lee Tourist Home ................................................ 712 E. 4th St.
Dallas
    Bogel Hotel ....................................................................... 821 Bogel St.
    Howard Hotel .............................................................. 3118 San Jacinto St.
    Lewis Hotel ................................................................ 302½ N. Central St.
    Powell Hotel ................................................................... 3115 State St.
    Y.M.C.A. ........................................................................ 2700 Flora St.
    Y.W.C.A. ........................................................................ 3525 State St.
    8th St. Motel ................................................................. 1937 8th St.
    Triple "A" Motel ........................................................... 1839 Ft. Worth Ave.
    2nd Ave. Motel .................................................................... 214 Long
    Green Acres Motel ........................................................ 1711 McCoy St.
    Palm Cafe Restaurant ................................................... 2213 Hall St.
    Shalimar Restaurant ..................................................... 2219 Hall St.
    Beaumont Barbeque Restaurant ................................. 1815 N. Field
El Paso
    Murray Theater Hotel .................................................. 218 S. Mesa Ave.
    Daniel Hotel ................................................................. 413 S. Oregon St.
    A. Winston Tourist Home .............................................. 3205 Almeda St.
    Mrs. S. W. Stull Tourist House ........................................ 511 Tornillo
    C. Williams Tourist Home ............................................. 1507 Wyoming St.
Fort Worth
    Y.M.C.A. ......................................................................... 1604 Jones St.
```

Started by New York City mailman Victor Hugo Green, the *Negro Motorist Green Book* became a critical tool for Blacks traveling through the South during the Jim Crow era (1936–1966). In this undated entry, the Inn of the Dove was known as the Triple "A" Motel. (Actual *Green Book* entry when the Dove Inn was Triple "A" Motel.)

The *Green Book* became known to the public after the success of the Academy Award-winning movie, *Green Book*, which chronicled the story of a Black pianist and white driver/bouncer as they traveled through the South in 1962.

After closing for several years, the hotel reopened in 2007 under the name Inn of the Dove. Although developers are encroaching on it and surrounding areas, so far, the owner has refused to sell.

THIS USED TO BE: Triple "R," Triple "A," Ranch Motel

NOW IT'S: Inn of the Dove

LOCATION: 1839 Ft. Worth Ave.

Babe Didrikson: "The Dallas Wonder"

The small, green frame house with lattice bordering its front porch doesn't look much different than the other residences in this part of Oak Cliff, an area of aging homes, most with only window-unit air conditioners and small backyards separated with chain fences and surrounded by prevalent but shabby-looking trees. The neighborhood grocery store, Fiesta, is a local chain that caters to the nearby significant Hispanic population. Little is noteworthy here, except that in the early 1930s, when the green house at 904 Haines St. was then barely a decade old, it was home to maybe America's greatest athlete, Babe Didrikson.

Didrikson could do it all: golf, basketball, track. She helped found the LPGA. (Courtesy of Wikipedia)

Didrikson excelled at virtually every sport: tennis, swimming, and golf. As a teen, she was recruited from her Beaumont home to play for Dallas's Employers Casualty Insurance Company (ECC) Golden Cyclones basketball team, which was in competition with the Dallas Sunoco Oilers, the company-sponsored women's AAU National Basketball Champions in 1927 and 1928.

ECC Coach Col. M. J. McCombs hired her as a secretary and to play basketball, with emphasis on the latter. The "secretarial job" paid $75 a week. It was a bargain.

From 1929 to 1933, Didrikson led the Golden Cyclones to one national title, two runner-up spots, and a fourth-place finish.

From 1929 to 1933, the Golden Cyclones set the record for most points in a tournament game (97) and the fewest allowed (four).

This nondescript Oak Cliff house is where Babe Didrikson lived in the early 1930s. She worked at Texas Employers Insurance. She was often seen playing golf at the nearby Stevens Golf Course. (Courtesy of Harry Hall.)

She single-handedly captured the 1932 AAU Track and Field Championship, winning six of 10 events, beating the 20-member runner-up team from Illinois, 30 points to 22. Later in the year, at the Los Angeles Olympic Games, Didrikson would score two golds and one silver in track, making her an international star and earning the nickname "The Dallas Wonder."

After the Olympics, Dallas held a parade in her honor and a reception that the *Dallas Morning News* said was bigger than the one that had greeted Charles Lindbergh on his 1927 Dallas visit.

THIS USED TO BE: Home to Babe Didrikson

NOW IT'S: A private residence

LOCATION: 904 Haines St.

The Statler Still Thrives

The Y-shaped, 19-story, modern-design Statler Hilton and Residences still stands tall at 1914 Commerce, its address since its inception in 1956. Staying true to its tagline, "The spirited lifestyle you crave," the 219 upper-floor apartments complement the hotel's 159 guestrooms. The rooms are larger than the original ones, and they offer all the modern amenities, such as mounted Smart HDTVs, Wi-Fi, Nespresso coffee makers, and a multiuse fitness center.

The Statler was created as a crown jewel in the hotel industry. It was the city's first major hotel in 30 years, and it received a grand kickoff as dignitaries from both coasts attended a four-day celebration. The $16 million structure had 1,000 rooms and was the largest convention center in the southwest. It had several hotel firsts, including elevator music and custom 21-inch televisions in every room, and it was among the first to have its 2,000-capacity ballroom and conference rooms on lower floors. There was even a heliport on the roof to shuttle guests from airports.

Over the years, the Statler changed names to Park Plaza and Dallas Grand Hotel before closing in 2001. It came close to destruction in 2007 and 2008, but was saved thanks to the work of Preservation Dallas. In 2008, the National Trust for Historic Preservation included the Statler Hilton on its list of "America's Most Endangered Places."

In 2017, Centurion American Development completed a three-year, $320 million upgrade as part of Hilton's Curio Collection division. While much was changed the outside, the blue-green glass, and porcelain-coated metal panels remain virtually untouched. All of its original terrazzo floors and marble touches on the walls have also been restored. The hotel has 10 spacious meeting rooms, with spectacular views of downtown Dallas.

Frank Sinatra, Styx, and Michael Jackson all performed in the Statler.

The Statler gives guests spectacular views of the Main Street Gardens, Texas State Fair, and the Farmers Market. Nearby attractions include entertainment, fine dining, shopping, and other varieties of Dallas nightlife. (https://creativecommons.org/licenses/by-sa/3.0/deed.en Photographer: Dfwcre8tive, Noah Jeppson.)

THIS USED TO BE: Statler Hilton Hotel

NOW IT'S: Statler Hotel and Residences

LOCATION: 1914 Commerce St.

Gables Republic Tower: More Than "The Rocket"

After 26 years, Republic Bank left the Davis Building and in 1954 moved into its own home, a spectacular 35-story aluminum and glass behemoth at 300 N. Ervay St. The massive structure made Republic Bank the tallest building in Dallas—topping rival Mercantile National Bank Building by 53 feet and beating out anything built west of the Mississippi River.

What added to its uniqueness and height was what stood atop the roof: a 150-foot spire, nicknamed "the rocket," has made the bank one of the most distinctive buildings in downtown Dallas. For years, at night a rotating beacon atop the rocket could be seen for a reported 120 miles.

For passersby and visitors, the rocket is the Republic Building, but what's inside might be even more noteworthy. Architects designed a column-free lobby expanse that would not be replicated today. To create it, the floors had to be hung from above. The lobby was finished with marble, inlaid wood, and 3,000 square feet of pure gold leaf. When it opened, conveniences included air-conditioning, 41 teller cages, with two reserved for women, and a motor bank in the basement.

Today, after a $75 million renovation, the Gables Republic Tower is now home to 229 residential units. It's close to several DART rail lines, the tunnel system, and additions that include penthouse floor plans and a theater room.

While the rocket remains a major attraction for the Gables, its stature has been diminished some, as taller buildings have reduced its skyline dominance and necessitated the elimination of the nocturnal rotating beacon. At night, it remains illuminated by floodlights.

The Gables Republic Tower is home to some of the nation's fastest elevators.

The 150-foot-high spire (aka the rocket) makes Republic Center one of the most distinctive buildings in Dallas. At one time, a rotating beacon atop the tower could reportedly be seen by planes more than 100 miles away. (https://creativecommons.org/licenses/by-sa/3.0/deed.en. Courtesy of Jeffrey Beall.)

THIS USED TO BE: Republic National Bank Building
NOW IT'S: Gables Republic Tower
LOCATION: 300 N. Ervay St.

A History of Dining Innovation and Convenience on Lower Greenville

The orange and red "Gloria's Restaurant" neon sign illuminating the maroon building immediately attracts the attention of anyone who passes it. Located in the heart of lower Greenville, one of Dallas's most popular dining areas, Gloria's Latin cuisine menu includes Salvadorian and Latin offerings such as pupusas, enchiladas, and tacos. *Dallas Travel Guide* even ranked Gloria's as a top 10 neighborhood restaurant. The atmosphere is semi-casual thanks to a pet-friendly patio and half-priced bottles of wine all day from Sunday to Tuesday.

That address was popular long before Salvadorian natives Gloria and Jose Fuentes opened Gloria's three decades ago. For years beginning in the 1930s, 3715 Greenville was home to Kirby's Pig Stand #4. If you've ever enjoyed Texas Toast, a chicken-fried steak sandwich, or onion rings, thank the Pig Stand Restaurant. In 1921, with Americans enjoying the increased mobility and convenience of the automobile, entrepreneur Jesse Kirby and Dr. Reuben Jackson created an idea for Dallasites to forego cooking and "Eat a Pig Sandwich," and they invented the world's first drive-in restaurant. The chain grew so popular that one advertisement boasted, "Join the 5,000 and avoid the bother of the evening meal." A lawsuit against copycat eateries led to a new restaurant design that "consisted of a red-tiled pagoda-like roof set on a rectangular building framed of wood and covered in stucco."

Pig Stands grew to 130 restaurants from California to New York. However, the rationing of supplies and gasoline during the Great Depression made running a business more difficult. Many Pig Stands were sold or went out of business.

Greenville's Pig Stand survived for years. While not achieving the success of its predecessor, Gloria's has expanded and developed a strong following. The day after a positive review in a Dallas paper, it saw a huge influx of new customers, including then-Governor Bill Clements.

With no experience, Gloria and Jose Fuentes, two Salvadorians who fled political unrest hoping to begin a new life in America, took over Gloria's sister's Oak Cliff restaurant. After many struggles, they began seeing success. Since the beginning 30 years ago, Gloria's has grown to 20 locations throughout Texas. (Photo by Harry Hall.)

Pig Stand hired the first carhops, lads who worked only for tips, so they jumped on the customers' running boards, often while the vehicles were still moving.

THIS USED TO BE: Pig Stand Restaurant

NOW IT'S: Gloria's Latin Cuisine

LOCATION: 3715 Greenville Ave.

The Bookstore That Encourages Conversation

The Wild Detectives Bookstore is a terra-cotta prairie-style converted World War II-era house located in Dallas's popular Bishop Arts District. It was once a major stop for the late 19th-century streetcars, but over the years became a virtual ghost town. A developer recognized its potential, and today many of the mom-and-pop shops that populate the area were once family residences, creating a nostalgic environment that is prevalent in Bishop Arts.

On Friday nights, customers feel and hear the creaky wooden floor under their feet. Some people sit and read while others engage in conversation. At the bar in back, patrons drink and talk. What you won't see is visitors wearing headphones, punching buttons, and staring at a screen. On weekends, WD is a "no Wi-Fi" zone. WD co-owners Paco Vique and Javier Garcia del Moral have created a bookstore unique from libraries or coffee shops. They want WD to be a place where people engage in intellectual conversation.

The two Spanish engineers met in Dublin, Ireland, in 2004, and they discovered a similar passion for books. Over the next decade, they ran into each other several times. In 2014, they found themselves in Dallas, determined it was "now or never," and opened The Wild Detectives.

Their philosophy of WD is rooted in 18th-century Europe, where coffee houses became popular places for literary discussion and advancements in thought and where strangers became friends. Although books dominate the store, a small bar sits in the back, recreating the old environment; the main goal is to get customers talking, which they believe is becoming a lost art.

"If you don't talk about books, they get forgotten," said Garcia del Moral at a TED Talk in 2016, "like poetry or classical music."

WD will order but won't deliver out-of-stock book requests. When you pick it up, the store buys you a drink.

Wild Detectives is not your typical bookstore. The converted World War II-era house has a bar in back and no Wi-Fi on weekends. The owners want to encourage conversation among their customers, creating an atmosphere similar to that of 18th-century Europe. (Photo by Harry Hall.)

THIS USED TO BE: A private residence

NOW IT'S: The Wild Detectives Bookstore

LOCATION: 314 West 8th

Eagle Ford School: The Last Remnant of Mexican American Pioneers

For decades, the aging Eagle Ford School sat alone, a red-bricked, gothic-revival building rotting on Chalk Hill Road, the final remnant of a virtually forgotten but important past. With shuttered windows and warped doors, it was frequently the target of vandals who took shots at the historically significant structure. Just to the east stands Cockrell Hill Road and Interstate 30, facing a series of restaurants and shops that dominate the once-blank landscape, but the school missed the revival.

Eagle Ford School was born out of necessity. Early in the 20th century, the nearby Trinity Cement Company hired 300 Mexican Americans who were fleeing political upheaval in Mexico. The immigrants needed jobs, and the cement company needed workers. The cement plant donated the land to build the school. It was completed in 1924, and it included a feature that most lacked in their homes, and few had probably ever seen: indoor plumbing.

By the mid-1950s, the Eagle Ford community was annexed into Dallas, the cement plant closed, and the school followed in 1965.

On the verge of destruction, several local organizations, led by the Dallas Mexican American Historical League, stepped in to save it.

Recently, new owners renovated the building, which among other problems had three feet of water standing in the basement. The outside and inside were restored their original design, down to the separate entries for boys and girls—genders were always segregated. There was not even intermingling for class pictures. The windows have been custom-designed and fitted as similar as possible to the original.

At the new school's open house, students returned after decades of seeing their childhood memory deteriorate. The restructured building will retain the name, but it has been converted for corporate events, weddings, and other special occasions.

A representative of the previous owner and an engineer said that the building was beyond repair, but after a significant upgrade, it seems ready to host a variety of private and corporate events. (Google Maps.)

The school is the only physical reminder of the communities Eagle Ford, Cemento Grande, and Arcadia Park. It's believed that Eagle Ford is the only remaining school in DISD in which students from a workers' village or "company town" attended. (Courtesy of Harry Hall.)

Bonnie Parker once attended school here.

THIS USED TO BE: Eagle Ford School

NOW IT'S: A place for meetings/events

LOCATION: 1601 Chalk Hill Rd.

Did Lone Star Lofts Serve as a SEAL Training Ground?

In November 2010, the interior of the proposed Lone Star Gas Lofts included kicked-in or demolished doors, broken glass, and walls peppered with powder burns and bullet holes. Shell casings littered the floor.

The 13-story Lone Star Gas Building, one of three that once made up the Atmos Complex and took up an entire city block inside Harwood, Wood, St. Paul, and Jackson Streets, had long been a place where customers paid their gas bills. Through the years, as fewer people conducted business downtown, the payment area was remodeled, becoming the company cafeteria, with the teller counter converted to a serving line. The ceiling was lowered, and fluorescent lights were added.

Beginning in 2013, renovation would eventually turn all three buildings into apartments. The website says the 230 lofts are "where Art Deco style meets modern luxurious living and inexpensive rents." While much has been upgraded, some early artifacts remain. Many of the bronze fixtures, including two large customer check desks, an ornate clock, and decorative railings, stand out. The original black porcelain water fountain and metal safe, located behind the teller counter, also remain along with lanterns and relief carvings depicting various elements of the natural gas industry.

But that renovation seemed an impossibility in late 2010, when rumors spread that Hamilton Properties Corp, a partner in the new facility, had rented the three buildings to the Naval Special Warfare Development Group, aka SEAL Team Six. In just a few months, the world would hear about the highly trained specialists who killed Osama bin Laden. But did the lofts really serve as the SEAL training ground? There's been no physical evidence, but stories have spread that some of the SEALs who trained in Dallas were among those assigned to that historic mission.

Rumors abound that the Lone Star Lofts, where customers once paid their gas bills, was part of the Navy SEAL training for those who killed Osama bin Laden. But questions linger: Why would an elite-trained force leave behind shell casings and targets? Would they use real ammo in their practice runs? (Courtesy of Harry Hall.)

"It's still overwhelming to think what went on here," says Ashley Farha, VP of Hamilton Properties Corp. "It really is like something out of a movie."

THIS USED TO BE: Possible training ground for SEAL mission that killed Osama bin Laden

NOW IT'S: Lone Star Lofts

LOCATION: 300 S. St. Paul

SOURCES

Where Bonnie Parker Made An Honest Living
Stone, Rachel, "Café Where Bonnie Parker Worked To Be New Restaurant," *The Lakewood Advocate*, January 26, 2015; Bosse, Paula, "Mrs. Hartgraves' Café, and Bonnie & Clyde Earning Paychecks on Swiss Avenue," *Flashback Dallas*, July 7, 2016.

The Mystery and Intrigue of Campisi's Restaurant (Egyptian Lounge)
"Why Campisi's is called the 'Egyptian Restaurant,' and Why People Claim it's Tied to the mob," The Dallas Whisperer, May 17, 2013; "A Dallas Restaurant Cashes in on Mob Connection," Fairbanks, Katie, *LA Times*, February 14, 1999; Campisi Menu.

The Home of Ray Charles
"Ray Charles' Style Formed in South Dallas Home," by David Flick, Pop Matters, March 5, 2007; "Ray Charles Lived Here, Now What?" by Robert Wilonsky, *Dallas Morning News*, September 2, 2018.

When Pegasus Dominated the Skyline
Granbury, Michael, "Dallas' Original Pegasus Restored and Rebuilt," *Dallas Morning News*, May 21, 2015; "The Red Flying Horse in Downtown/Pegasus," The Dallas Whisperer, March 26, 2013; omnihotels.com, "Pegasus Lands at the Omni Dallas Hotel; Kallos, Kay," Dallas Gateway "Magnolia's Flying Red Horse," February 22, 2018.

Dry Above, Wet Underground
Rogers, Tom, "Why Dakota's is Called Dakota's," *D Magazine*, July 16, 2010; Neathery, Cody, "Three Decades Later, Dallas' Underground Steakhouse Keeps the Menu Fresh," *Dallas Observer*, February 29, 2016.

When Winfrey Point Served as a POW Camp
Trube, Emily, "Members of Hitler's Army on the Shores of White Rock Lake," KRLD Radio 1080, March 21, 2014; "About White Rock Lake," whiterockboatclub.com/about-white-rock-lake; Camp White Rock Site; "Gone, But Not Forgotten…" www.watermelon-kid.com/places/wrl/gone/gone_ccc-camp.html.

From "Ho, Ho, Ho!" to "Howdy, Folks!"
Wilkins, Amanda, "Howdy, folks: 10 things you probably didn't know about Big Tex," www.guidelive.com/state-fair/2015/09/24/howdy…, September 24, 2015; "Howdy, Folks, This is Big Tex!" State Fair of Texas, 2019.

For Dallas Blacks, the Pythias Temple Had It All
Govenar, Alan and Brakefield, Jay, *Deep Ellum: The Other Side of Dallas*, (Texas A&M University Press 2013), pp. 37–44; Wilonsky, Robert, "Knight's Tale," *Dallas Observer*, December 20, 2007; Copeland, Alex, "Knights of Pythias Temple in Deep Ellum," centraltrack.com, August 2, 2017; Wilonsky, Robert, "Getting History Back Will Haunt Us," *Dallas Morning News*, June 13, 2018.

Where Dallasites Watched the DJs Work
Offshore Radio Museum, KLIF Dallas, offshoreradiomuseum.co.uk/page895.html; "History of KLIF, Part 2," www.klifhistory.com/history-of-klif-part-2.

Dallas Bar Association Buys the Belo Mansion
"Belo Mansion, About," www.belomansion.com; "A History of the Belo Mansion & Dallas Bar Association," "Renting the Building," "Booking a Meeting Room," "Belo Mansion Lunch Buffet," dallasbar.org.

It Will Always Be the Texas School Book Depository
Nall, Matthew Hayes, "Texas School Book Depository," Texas State Historical Association, uploaded on June 15, 2010; "History of the Texas School Book Depository Building," JFK Museum, www.jfk.org; editors of *Encyclopedia Britannica*, "Lee Harvey Oswald, American Accused Assassin."

Crockett School Part of Neighborhood Revitalization
Brown, Steve, Real Estate Editor, "Spooky Old East Dallas Elementary School Will Get New Life As Apartments," *Dallas Morning News,* September 23, 2016; Maddox, Will, "This 114-Year Old School Building in the Neighborhood Could Be Your Next Residence," *Lakewood Advocate,* October 6, 2017; Brown, Steve, Real Estate Editor, "Old Dallas School Will Get New Life as Urban Rental Community," *Dallas Morning News,* October 5, 2017; Video, "Has Davy Crockett School Been Forgotten?" video by Ryan Cabrera, Kara DioGuardi, John Shanks, https://www.youtube.com/watch?v=SLIrUJD5wMs.

When WWI Pilots Trained in Dallas
Marie, Rose, "LT Moss Lee Love obituary," Find a Grave Memorial #29313576 Fairfax City Cemetery Fairfax, Fairfax City, VA Maintained, *Love Notes History;* "Chronology of Events," *Love Notes;* LT Moss Lee Love, Dallas Airport System, City of Dallas Aviation Dept; Army "Aviator is Killed Instantly at San Diego," *The Bakersfield Californian,* September 4, 1913; "Dallas Love Field Total Passengers, December 2008," City of Dallas Aviation Dept.

New Technology Replaces Cobb Stadium
Miller, Rich, "The Equinox Infomart: What It Means for the Data Center Industry," www.datacenterfrontier.com, Kaul, Greta, "Vignettes of Buildings in 'Lost Dallas, *Dallas Morning News,* July 14, 2012; "1967-1981 Dallas Tornado," funwhileitlasted.net, December 16, 2011; Doty, Mark, *Lost Dallas (Images of America)* (Arcadia Press) p. 123.

Musical History Made at 508 Park Avenue
"Encore Park Presents 508 Park," "508 Park's Historical Overview," 508park.org; Darling, Cary, "Step into Dallas' Historic 508 Park Building, Now Becoming Encore Park," *Fort Worth Star-Telegram,* March 4, 2015; Wilonsky, Robert, "Robert Johnson's Dallas Recording Studio Gets Pulled From Purgatory," *Dallas Morning News,* May 5, 2011.

Antebellum Mansion Moved to Old City Park
Rumbley, Rose Mary, *The Unauthorized History of Dallas, Texas, The Scenic Route Through 150 Years in 'Big D,'* (Eakin Press, Austin, TX 1991) p. 158; Stuertz, Mark, *Secret Dallas: A Guide to the Weird, Wonderful and Obscure,* (Reedy Press, 2018) pp. 22-23.

Dallas's Top Outdoor Dining Experience?
"The St. Ann Building," from "The Samurai Collection," Wilson, Lindsey, "St. Ann Restaurant & Bar Beckons Dallas Drinkers During Patio Season," by Culture Map Dallas, March 14, 2014; Rienstra, Jonathan, "The 10 Best Patios in Dallas to Soak Up the Sun," Culture Map Dallas, March 20, 2013; Reiss, Sarah, "First Take Review: St. Ann Restaurant and Bar," *D Magazine,* November 13, 2013.

Slave Descendants Delivered from Little Egypt
"Little Egypt Families Leave Shacks for Modern Homes," AP story, *Albuquerque Journal,* NM, May 16, 1962; Christina Hughes Babb, Christina Hughes, "Lake Highlands History Lesson: Little Egypt," *Lake Highlands Advocate,* August 2, 2011; Young, Michael E., "Life Was Hard in Freedman's Town Called Little Egypt," *Dallas Morning News,* February 24, 2002; Babb, Christina Hughes, "Do You Remember 'Little Egypt?' If So, You could Help 'Rebuild' It," *Lake Highlands Advocate,* September 21, 2015.

Kidd Springs Park: A Great Place for Families and Feasting
"The Barbeque Chronicles: Blues, Bandits and BBQ Festival, the Posse's First Cookoff," texasbbqposse.com October, 2010; Stone, Rachel, "Best of 2019 Voting," *Oak Cliff Advocate* November 8, 2016; "Kidd Springs Park," courtesy of Friends of Oak Cliff Parks, 2017; "Blues, Bandits, and BBQ," Don O.'s Texas Barbeque Blog, 2018.

Texas's Only Playboy Club
Downs, Catherine, "Playboy Bunnies Tell the Best Tales," *D Magazine,* September 2018; Gallagher, Danny, "Where They Felt Protected," *Dallas Observer,* October 4, 2017; Heckman, Paul, "Playboy of Dallas," MemoriesofDallas.org; Wynn, Christopher, "A Look Back at Dallas' Playboy Club, Including Hugh Hefner's Strobe-Flash Visit," Arts and Culture Editor, *Dallas Morning News,* July 27, 2012.

The Many Villages of Sam Ventura
Bosse, Paula, "Sam Ventura's Italian Village, Oak Lawn," *Flashback: Dallas*.

Streetcars Transform Jefferson Street
Stone, Rachel, "History: When Jefferson at Tyler Was the Center of the Oak Cliff Universe," *Oak Cliff Advocate*, August 2016.

Multiple Lives of the Davis Building
"History of the Davis Building," http://thedavisbuilding.com; "Historic Dallas Tower is Preserved and Reborn," https://www.colorkinetics.com/global/showcase/davis-building; "Drakestone," https://www.rentcafe.com/apartments/tx/dallas/the-davis-building/default.aspx.

Pedestrian Bridge Gives Underserved Families Recreational Opportunity
"Continental Avenue Bridge and West Dallas Gateway" from https://trinityrivercorridor.com/recreation/continental-ave-bridge; "Our Story, Klyde Warren Park, Dallas, Texas," from klydewarrenpark.org; Castillo, Gregory, "All Day Party Celebrates Continental Bridge Reopening," *Dallas Morning News* June 15, 2014.

Carnegie Brings Libraries to Dallas
Brooks, Gayla, "History: The Oak Cliff Library's Wealthy Heritage," *Oak Cliff Advocate*, October 2013; *The WPA Dallas Guide and History*, (published by the Dallas Public Library and the UNT Press, 1992), pp.80, 230, 359.

Has Tragedy Kept the Texas Theatre Alive?
"About-the Texas Theatre," thetexastheatre.com/about.

What Is the Future of Dallas's First Motor Hotel?
"History of Belmont Hotel Dallas," http://www.belmontdallas.com/belmont-dallas-hotel-history.php; "New Management Sees Big Future for Remodeled Belmont Motor Hotel," *Dallas Morning News*, June 20, 1965, updated by Robert Wilonsky via scribd.com; Wilonsky, Robert, "As West Dallas' Iconic Belmont Hotel Grows Sad and Shabby, a Push To Make it a Historic Landmark," *Dallas Morning News*, March 22, 2019.

Jump-Starting the West End Marketplace
Heid, Jason, "Ghosts of Dallas: Spaghetti Warehouse, 1977," *D Magazine*, December 18, 2013; "Spaghetti Warehouse," https://www.dallaswestend.org/members/spaghetti-warehouse/; "Spaghetti Warehouse-Dallas" via PANICd.

The Home of Dallas's Bandit Queen
Acheson, Sam, "Belle Starr. The Bandit Queen," *Dallas Morning News*, January 9, 1967; Tolbert, Frank X. "Tolbert's Texas, Belle Starr Street Finally Spelled Right," *Dallas Morning News*, August 3, 1976; "Myra Shirley Belle Starr," *Dallas Morning News*, February 13, 1889; Rogers, John William, *The Lusty Texans of Dallas*, (E. P. Dutton and Company, NY 1960), pp 147-153.

Beyond Its German Roots
Schilo, Fritz, "Sons of Hermann," "Texas State Historical Association," A (Not So) Brief History," https://www.sonsofhermannhall.com/our-history; "Sons of Hermann Hall," outhousetickets.com; "Dallas General Assorted History," *Dallas Gateway*, March 21, 2018.

Concrete Viaduct Replaces Washed-Out Wooden Bridge
"Houston Street Viaduct," Waymarking.com; Payne, Darwin, *Big D Triumphs and Troubles of an American Supercity in the 20th Century*, (Three Forks Press, Dallas, 1994) pp 21-25; "The Great Dallas Flood of 1908," from The Historians Abode, October 31, 2008; "Dallas General Assorted History," *Dallas Gateway*, February 10, 2018; "Bridge, Houston St, Dallas," Texas Historical Commission.

A Beer Baron Upends City Hall
Acheson, Sam, "First Dallas Municipal Building" courtesy of Yesterday Dallas, *Dallas Gateway*, April 9, 2018, https://dallasgateway.com/first-dallas-city-hall-liveliest-joint/; Childers, Sam and the City of Dallas, Historic Dallas Hotels,"; Fitzgerald, Ken, "Dallas Then and Now," *Dallas Gateway*, March 16, 2018.

Exchange Park Advances Dallas Business Atmosphere
"Lost + Found: Exchange Park: 1950's Cutting Edge," www.diadallas.org, "Braniff History Today," by Richard Cass, braniffboutique.com/blogs/braniff-history-today/braniff-history-today-1-22-56, January 22, 1956; inside help/interview from Michael Sarelli, UT SW Medical Center.

West Dallas Finally Connects to Mainstream Dallas
Simek, Peter, "Trinity Groves: The New Dallas Starts Here," *D Magazine*, January 2013; Brenner, Leslie, "Your Table Awaits, Diners Have a Panoply of Choices at Trinity Groves, With So Many More to Come," *DMN Interactives: Trinity Groves, A Dining Theme Park*, January 31, 2014; "West Dallas: Trinity Groves," *Visit Dallas: Big Things Happen Here*.

Spanish Flu Derails Military Training Camp
Bosse, Paula, "Preston Sturges: Camp Dick's Most Famous Former Cadet?" *Flashback: Dallas*, November 13, 2016; *The WPA Dallas Guide and History*, (published by the Dallas Public Library and the University of North Texas Press, 1992), p. 88; Leatherwood, Art, "Camp John Dick Aviation Concentration Camp," *Handbook of Texas* Online, accessed April 7, 2019; Anderson, Jennifer, "On This Day in Dallas: October 12, 1918, Mayor Lawther Bans All Public Gatherings in Effort to Slow Spread of Spanish Flu," City of Dallas Historic Preservation Program, October 12, 2018/November 27, 2018.

Dallas Welcomes the Fair Park Fire Station
"Dallas Fire Fighter's Museum Facts," www.dallasfiremuseum.com; "Building History," www.dallasfiremuseum.com; "the Fire Station at Fair Park has Served with Distinction for Almost a Century," www.dallasfiremuseum.com; "Old Tige," www.dallasfiremuseum.com.

Hotel St. Germain Sets the Standard for Excellence
Heap, Kristiana, "European Elegance on Millionaires Row; Local Landmark Celebrates Double Anniversary," Society Editor, *PeopleNewspapers.com*; Mariani, John, "Two New Dining Rooms in Big D," Virtual Gourmet Newsletter Vol. IV, No. 7; "2009 Dallas Restaurant Design Awards, Best Silverware," *D Magazine*, November 2009; "Dining Room at the Hotel St. Germain," 10best.com.

Doak Walker Plaza Honors a Legend
Merwin, John, "Where Have You Gone, Doak Walker?" *D Magazine*, August 1977; "About Doak Walker," www.smu.edu/DoakWalkerAward/AboutUs/AboutDoakWalker; "Washington Running Back Wins First Doak Walker Award," *The Jackson Sun* (TN), December 8, 1990; "Enhancing the Campus Environment: Mustang Plaza and Mall," blog.smu.edu, April, 2010.

The Unlikely Revival of the Filter Building
"History of White Rock Lake and the Filter Building," thefilterbuilding.com; "The Boathouse," whiterockrowing.org/the/boathouse.

Farmers Market District: Symbol of Dallas Growth
"Dallas Farmers Market," *Dallas Gateway*, November 7, 2018; Dallas Farmer's Market, Cultivating Life, dallasfarmersmarket.org; "Mudhen Meat and Greens," www.mudheninthe.net.

The Sportatorium: Host of Pro Wrestling and the King of Rock 'n' Roll
Dilbert, Ryan, "Dallas Sportatorium, the Mecca of Pro Wrestling in Texas," bleacherreport.com/articles/2561329-dallas, October 21, 2015; "If Those Walls Could Talk," https://prowrestlingstories.com/pro-wrestling-stories/dallas-wrestling-sportatorium/; Limon, Elvira, "What Happened to the 'World Famous' Sportatorium? Texas Goes Back in Time," Curious Texas, *Dallas Morning News*, February 2, 2019.

The One-Time Coffin Company Now Offers Luxury
Alsobrook, Adam, "Resting Place," Project Reviewer, Division of Architecture, *Texas Historical Commission*, submitted by Rob Hodges, December 18, 2012; "Grand Opening," video of debut of CANVAS Hotel, February 28, 2019.

The Southwest's Greatest Playground
Rogers, Kenneth Horan, *The Lusty Texans of Dallas*, (E. P. Dutton and Co. NY, 1960) pp 209-213; Brooks, Gayla, "Oak Cliff History: How Our Neighborhood Came to be," *The Oak Cliff Advocate*, April 28, 2014.

This Gas Station Housed A Killer
Rumbley, Rose-Marie, *The Unauthorized History of Dallas, Texas, The Scenic Route Through 150 Years in "Big D,"* (Eakin Press, Austin, TX, 1991) p 144-145; Rosenberg, Jennifer, "Biography of Bonnie and Clyde, Notorious Depression-Era Outlaws," Thought Co., July 24, 2019.

Arts Magnet School Earns National Acclaim
"About Booker T. Washington HSPVA," https://www.dallasisd.org/domain/3088; "History of Booker T. Washington for the Performing and Visual Arts," https://www.dallasisd.org/domain/233; Payne, Darwin, *Big D, Triumphs and Troubles of an American Super City in the 20th Century,* (Three Forks Press, Dallas 1994) p 69; interview with Katie Bernet, Booker T. Washington graduate.

The Brothers Who Redefined the Retail Industry
"About El Centro College," https://www.elcentrocollege.edu/au/pages/default.aspx; Kleiner, Diana J., "Sanger Brothers," *Handbook of Texas Online,* uploaded June 15, 2010; Anderson, Jennifer, "Sanger Brothers in Dallas," *City of Dallas Historic Preservation Program,* November 8, 2018.

When Blacks and Whites Lived in Different Worlds
Ragland, James, "Old Forest Avenue Alumni Celebrate Dallas School's Heritage Look to Future," *Dallas Gateway,* courtesy of Ragland, *Dallas Morning News,* October 25, 2012; Forest assigned to Negro pupils: District added to Crozier's, *Dallas Morning News,* June 14, 1956.

The Theater That Wouldn't Stay Down
"Best Live Music Venue: Kessler Theater," *Dallas Observer,* 2014; Metcalf, Jessica, "The Kessler: An Art Deco for Music Lovers," www.texashomesforsale.com/articles/thekessler-theater; Appleton, Roy, "Kessler Theater Building Gains Listing on National Register of Historic Places," www.dallasnews.com/news/oak-cliff.

Old Mill Restaurant Maintains Nostalgic Character
Rumbley, Rose-Mary, *The Unauthorized History of Dallas, Texas, The Scenic Route Through 150 Years in 'Big D,'* (Eakin Press, Austin, TX 1991) p. 166; Campbell, Ed, "History of the Old Mill Inn," www.oldmillinn-fairparkdallas.tx.com/history.html; "Old Mill Inn," *Dallas Gateway,* February 28, 2018; "Drop by to: Dine, Drink, Deduce, Die…Laughing," Keith and Margo's Ultimate Mystery Dinner Adventure," murdermysterytexas.com/locations/dallas/old-mill-inn-2.

America's Most Decorated Soldier Owned This Farmhouse
Beaubien, Adam and Elizabeth, Owners of Dovie's "About," (Dovie's), https://pbdallas.com/moreinfo/dovies-350; "America's Most Decorated WWII Combat Soldier, Audie L. Murphy_Memorial_Website;" Places to Visit, Homes Owned or Lived in by Audie Murphy," Audie L Murphy Memorial Website; Note: Memorial website has been suspended.

A Tragedy That Transformed the World's Health
Hall, Cheryl, "Aerobics Pioneer Still in the Fitness Business at 86," *Dallas Morning News,* July 2, 2017; Thompson, Whitney, "The Making of a Health and Wellness Empire," *Lakewood/East Dallas Advocate,* July 28, 2014; Kufahl, Pamela, "Dr. Kenneth Cooper and How He Became the Father of Aerobics," Editor-in-Chief, clubindustry.com.

Attention-Getting Billboard
Hurley, Jennifer, "This Billboard is so Awesome-Dallas Made It a Landmark," Look up, Clear Channel Outdoor Blog, September 21, 2017; "Famous Waterfall Billboard Near Downtown Dallas Gets Artist's Makeover," https://www.wfaa.com/article/news/local/famous-waterfall-billboard-near-downtown-dallas-gets-artists-makeover/443293500, May 26, 2017; Limon, Elvia, "What's the Story Behind Dallas' Famous Waterfall Billboard? Curious Texas Dips Into History," *Dallas Morning News,* January 3, 2019.

Parkland Memorial Hospital Moves Forward
"Parkland's History," https://www.parklandhospital.com/parklands-history; "General Information," https://www.parklandhospital.com/parklands-history; "New Centralized Burn Center," https://www.parklandhospital.com/parklands-history.

Dallas's First Home
"John Neely Bryan Cabin," by *NW History Buff,* February 10, 2017; "John Neely Bryan, Founder of Dallas," the Robinson Library, last updated December 24, 2017; Rogers, John Williams, *Lusty*

Texans of Dallas, (E. P. Dutton and Company, NY 1960), pp 54-55; *The WPA Dallas Guide and History*, (published by the Dallas Public Library and the University of North Texas Press, 1992) pp. 38-40, 44.

Harper Jr., Cecil, "Bryan, John Neely," *Handbook of Texas Online*, uploaded on June 12, 2010.

A Cook-Off That Inspired an International Restaurant Chain
Smith, Dominique, "Ten Reasons Why Chili's is the Best," *Odyssey*, December 19, 2016; "15 Little-Known Facts About Chili's," www.menuism.com/articles/15-little-known-factslabout-chili's-1020; Best Junk Food, *D Magazine*, August 1982; Yagalla, Mark, "A Few Things You Might Not Know About Chili's," www.fool.com, December 7, 2013.

Has the Continental Gin Building Gone Bust?
"Burton Farmer's Gin," https://www.asme.org/wwwasmeorg/media/resourcefiles/aboutasme/who%20we%20are/engineering%20history/landmarks/173-burton-farmers-gin-mill-1914.pdf, April 15, 1994; Robert Sylvester Munger, *Handbook of Texas Online*, via *Dallas Morning News*, April 21, 1923, uploaded June 15, 2010; Bosse, Paula, "Munger's Improved Continental Gin Company," *Flashback: Dallas*, February 24, 2015; Pesquera, Adolfo, "In a Changing Deep Ellum, the Continental Gin Building Faces the Future," https://dallas.towers.net, August 23, 2018.

From Old Red Courthouse to Museum
"Building Highlights;" Old Red Museum of Dallas County History and Culture; "Old Red Courthouse Defies Critics," *Dallas Gateway*, June 18, 2018; "The Story of Dallas County Begins Here," "Old Red Museum of Dallas County History and Culture," oldred.org.

Tootsies Continues Predecessor's High Standards
Nicholson, Eric, "A Glimpse at the Old Preston Center Neiman Marcus," *Preston Hollow People* June 11, 2010; "Neiman Marcus-The Christmas Catalog-His and Hers and Fantasy Gifts," http://www.liquisearch.com/neiman_marcus/the_christmas_catalog/his_and_hers_amp_fantasy_gifts; "About Us," www.tootsies.com.

Musical Venue Expands, But Remains True to Its Roots
"Our World Famous Brunch Even Raises the Roof," www.houseofblues.com/dallas/gospelbrunch, Brown, Steve, "Dallas' House of Blues Building in Victory Park Sold to New York Investor," *Dallas Morning News*, April 12, 2013; Perez, Christine, "House of Blues Dallas Building on the Market for $18 Million," www.dmagazine.com, July 12, 2012.

DART Preserves Monroe Shops
"DART Police to Take Over Rail Maintenance Facility," www.metro-magazine.com, March 21, 2011; Wilonsky, Robert, "Wherein We Throw Some Items at the DART Board to See if The Stick," *Dallas Observer*, March 9, 2010; Hudson, Travis, "DART Police Headquarters Celebrates 100th Birthday," dartdallas.dart.org, July 30, 2014; "DART's Historic Structural Renovation," www.buildingenclosureonline.com, July 1, 2013.

The Ladies of Frogtown
Payne, Darwin, B*ig D, Triumphs and Troubles of an American Super City in the 20th Century*, (Three Forks Press, Dallas 1994), pp 41-48; "A City Founded on Hard Justice," *D Magazine*, March 2018; Crowell, Gwinnetta Malone, "Not in My Backyard, 'Legalizing Prostitution in Dallas from 1910-1913'" Dallas Historical Legacies, *A History Journal for Dallas and North Central Texas*, Volume 22, Number 2, Fall 2010.

Woodruff Robbed of Record?
Litsky, Frank, "A Victory That's Still Memorable 70 Years Later," *New York Times*, August 1, 2006; "Greater Texas and Pan American Exposition Index," http://www.watermelon-kid.com/places/FairPark/panam/panam_intro.htm; Finder, Chuck, "70 years ago today, Connellsville native John Woodruff Sprinted from Last to First to Win Gold at Berlin Olympics, *Pittsburgh Post-Gazette*, August 4, 2006; "John Woodruff, National Visionary," *National Visionary Leadership Project*.

Dallas Moves the Trinity River
Furlong, John N., Ajemian, Greg PE, and McPherson, Ms. Tommie, PE "History of the Dallas Floodway, ASCE Meeting, Fall, 2003; Bosse, Paula, "The Trinity at the City's Doorstep," *Flashback:*

Dallas, June 24, 2014; Halford, Lee, "Leslie Allison Stemmons," *Dallas County Pioneer Association's Proud Heritage*, Volume 3, February 17, 2018.

Lucky Lindy's Reputation Nosedives
Peppard, Alan, "Lone Eagle Lindbergh in Dallas' First Ticker-Tape Parade," *Dallas Morning News*, August 7, 2013; Stone, Rachel, "How Lindbergh Drive Became Skillman," *The Lakewood/East Dallas Advocate*, December 7, 2011; Fink, Jack, "A Look Back at the History of Dallas Love Field," CBSDFW.COM, October 10, 2014.

Dallas's Last Vaudeville House
"Iconic Downtown Dallas Building; The Majestic Theatre," by Parks for Downtown Dallas, May 26, 2017; Caldwell, Shirley, "Majestic Theatre," "A Guide to the History of Dallas, TX;" Majestic Theatre (Dallas), *Handbook of Texas Online*, uploaded June 15, 2010, updated May 2, 2016.

Cumberland School Makes Huge Transformation
"Jesse Jones Attended Cumberland Hill," *Gateway Dallas*, November 25, 2018; Dallas Little Mexico School, *Gateway Dallas*, February 18, 2018; Cumberland Hill School, *A Guide To the History of Dallas, Texas*, updated January 13, 2011.

Interurban Rail Creates Progress in Transportation
Jensen, Jerimiah, "AT&T Buys Historic Interurban Building," *D Magazine*, January 11, 2019; Magers, Michael, The Interurban (Texas Electric Railway), *The Texas Story Project*, February 3, 2015; "Luxury Living in Downtown Dallas," https://www.interurbanbuilding.com/home.aspx.

The Colorful Legacy of the Longhorn Ballroom
Nichols, Nancy, "Does Anyone but Me Remember O. L. Nelms?" *D Magazine*, August 28, 2007; "Longhorn Legacy," https://www.longhornballroom.com/history/; "The Historic Longhorn Ballroom," https://www.longhornballroom.com/history/, Wilonsky, Robert, "From Bob Wills to Jack Ruby, Dallas' Longhorn Ballroom has History Worth Saving and New Life Worth Celebrating," *Dallas Morning News*, February 10, 2017.

Dying 110-Year-Old School Gets New Life
Chu, Christy, "Former Dallas High School in Transition," *Shells of Our City*, April 23, 2012; "Perkins + Will Moves Offices to Historic Dallas High School Building," *Towers*, December 7, 2017; Carlisle, Candace, "History Reborn: an Exclusive Look inside the 108 year old Dallas High School Building," *Dallas Business Journal*, August 14, 2015.

Will Millennials Hang Out at This Former A-List Hotel?
Evans, Candy, "Mehrdad Moayedi Buying, Reviving Cabana Motor Hotel Where Beatles Stayed: Hotel, Pools, Bars," CandysDirt.com, October 6, 2017; Prezoisi, David, contributor, "Lost + Found: Cabana Motor Hotel," https://www.aiadallas.org.

The Lakewood Theater Is Spared
Macon, Alex, "A Bowling Alley-Bar is Coming to the Lakewood Theater," *D Magazine*, July 24, 2018; Dunaway, Jaime, "Bowling Alley Takes Shape in the Historic Lakewood Theater," *Lakewood/East Dallas Advocate*, May 7, 2019; Gray, Kevin, "The Lakewood Theater Strikes Again," *Hot List*, Summer 2019; Nunn, Brittany and Mitchell, Keri, "What Will Become of the Lakewood Theater?" *Lakewood/East Dallas Advocate*, December 29, 2014.

When Dallas Put Trains Underground
"Dallas Landmark Nomination Form," https://dallascityhall.com/departments/sustainabledevelopment/historicpreservation.

A Major Golf Tournament Got Its Start Here
"The Purpose of the Club is to Provide Social and Recreational Activities for its Members," Lifestyle-Lakewood Country Club, www.lakewoodcc.com/about/lifestyle; "Membership," "Lakewood Country Club," www.lakewoodcc.com/membership; "Texas Victory Open 1944 WRR Dallas," (audio) Byron Nelson, Harold "Jug" McSpaden, Ben Hogan, Ray Mangrum, https://www.youtube.com/watch?v=Dzp-34vkPpU&t=11s; Charrier, Emily, "Lakewood Country Club," *Lakewood/East Dallas Advocate*, June 14, 2017.

It Really Was a Bomb Factory, Sort of
Wood, Matt, "Remembering the Bomb Factory's Original Run With the Dallas Observer

Archives," *The Dallas Observer*, March 26, 2015; "Ford Assembly Plant in East Dallas," by Advocate Staff, *Lakewood/East Dallas Advocate*, June 1, 1998.

Plans for Cedars Development Go Up in Smoke
Venkatraman, Sakshi, "The Ambassador Hotel, a Dallas Landmark in the Cedars, Demolished After Fire," *D Magazine*, May 28, 2019; Brunfield, Loyd, "Crews Demolish Face of Ambassador After Fire Destroys Dallas' Oldest Hotel," Breaking News Producer, *Dallas Morning News*, May 28, 2019; Murray, Lance, "First Look: The Ambassador Hotel Redevelopment in the Cedars," https://dallasinnovates.com, January 30, 2018.

The First International Hotel Chain Started in Dallas
"Conrad Hilton Biography: The History of Hilton Hotels Corporation," Astrum People (2019), January 5, 2019.

The French-Influenced Wilson Building
Heid, Jason, "Ghosts of Dallas: H. L Green Protest 1960," *D Magazine*, December 18, 2014; Payne, Darwin, *Big D, Triumphs and Troubles of an American 20th Century Supercity in the 20th Century*, pp 299-300; 365; Acheson, Sam, "J. B. Wilson Brands Iconic Building," "Dallas Yesterday," via *Dallas Gateway*," May 2, 2018; Rumbley, Rose-Mary, *The Unauthorized History of Dallas, Texas, The Scenic Route Through 150 Years in 'Big D,'* (Eakin Press, Austin, TX 1991) p. 63.

Dallas World Aquarium: More Than Fish
"About the Dallas World Aquarium," https://dwazoo.com/about-dwa/; "Exhibits," www.dwazoo.com/exhibits.

Don't Mess with My Tex-Mex
"El Fenix Celebrates a Century of Tex-Mex," by RestaurantNews.com, February 27,2018; Lenzmier, Trevor, "America's Oldest Tex-Mex Chain Rings In 100 with Enchiladas and Excitement," *Chain Restaurants*, February 2018. Blaskovich, Sarah, "For 100 Years, El Fenix has Defined, Tex-Mex," *Dallas Morning News*, September 13, 2018.

Not the Cowboys "Field of Dreams"
Osborne, Ryan, "Willie Mays, the DFW Rangers and 'Jabbo:' the Story of a Forgotten Baseball Stadium," https://www.wfaa.com/article/news/willie-mays-the-dfw-rangers-and-jabbo-the-story-of-a-forgotten-baseball-stadium/287-533033955, March 28, 2018; Townsend, Brad, "Cowboys Practice Facilities Have Come a Long Way From Rat-infested Minor-League Park," *Dallas Morning News*, August 15, 2016; Stone, Rachel, Oak Cliff History: Our Neighborhood was Home to pro Baseball for about 50 years," *Oak Cliff Advocate*, March, 2015.

The Little Oak Cliff Store That Grew to Worldwide Prominence
Stone, Rachel, "Oak Cliff History: Oak Cliff is the Birthplace of 7-Eleven," the *Oak Cliff Advocate*, January 25, 2016; Rumbley, Rose-Mary, *The Unauthorized History of Dallas, Texas, The Scenic Route Through 150 Years in 'Big D,'* (Eakin Press, Austin, TX 1991) p 89; Encyclopedia Britiannica, "7-Eleven," https://www.britiannica.com/topic/7-Eleven.

Women's Center Honors One of Dallas's Great Ones
England, Joanna, "Ebby's Place Beyond The Little White House: YWCA Names Women's Center After Dallas' Grand Dame of Real Estate," CandysDirt.com, March 6, 2014; Frequently Asked Questions About WiNGS," by "WiNGS Dallas," https://wingsdallas.org/for-women/faq/; "Welcome to the WiNGS Center at Ebby's Place Where Women Come to Create Their Path to a Better Future," https://wingsdallas.org/for-women/faq/.

Inn of the Dove Was a Godsend for Blacks
Wilonsky, Robert, A Piece of the History Behind Oscars Best Picture Winner, 'Green Book,' Still Stands in West Dallas," *Dallas Morning News*, February 25, 2018.

Babe Didrikson: "The Dallas Wonder"
Bosse, Paula, "Babe Didrikson, Oak Cliff Typist," *Flashback: Dallas*, November 16, 2014; *The WPA Dallas Guide and History*, (published by the Dallas Public Library and the University of North Texas Press, 1992) pp 316-317; Lewis, Jone Johnson, "History of Women's Basketball in America, a Timeline of Women's Basketball History 1891-Present," Brooks, Gayla, https://www.thoughtco.com/history-of-womens-basketball-in-america-3528489, updated June 21, 2018; "Gold Mined in the Cliff," *Oak Cliff Advocate*, September 26, 2012.

The Statler Still Thrives
"Event Calendar," http://thestatlerdallas.com/events/; "The Statler Dallas Curio Collection by Hilton," https://www.guestreservations.com/the-statler-dallas-curio-collection-by-hilton/booking/: "Something Greater, History," https://tehstatlerdallas.com/somethinggreter/.

Gables Republic Tower: More Than "The Rocket"
Bosse, Paula, "The Republic National Bank Building: Miles of Aluminum, Gold Leaf, and a Rocket," *Flashback: Dallas*, April 25, 2014; "Republic Center History, In the Beginning," https://www.republiccenter.com/culture_history.html; "Republic Center Destination, Heart of the City," https://www.republiccenter.com/culture_downtown.html.

A History of Dining Innovation and Convenience on Lower Greenville
Jacobs, Ilene, "Take a Culinary Tour Around Greenville Avenue's Coolest Eateries," *Dallas Travel Guide*, May 26, 2016; Baird, Bill, "Dallas Pig Stands Quietly Vanished," *Gateway Dallas*, September 4, 2018; "A Little History About the Founding of Gloria's Restaurants," from Gloria's Restaurants Blog, February 18, 2011.

The Bookstore That Encourages Conversation
"About the Wild Detectives," https://thewilddetectives.com/about/; Smith, David Hale, "Return of the Great American Indie Bookstore, the Demise of the Neighborhood Readers' Paradise has Been Greatly Exaggerated," *The American Way*, February, 2015; "Interview with a Bookstore: The Wild Detectives, Uniting Books and Beer," *Literary Hub, The Guardian*, August 15, 2016; Del Moral, Javier Garcia, "Why Did We Add a Bar to Our Book Store?" TED Talk, Arlington, TX, April 1, 2016.

Eagle Ford School: The Last Remnant of Mexican American Pioneers
Wilonsky, Robert, "A Rush to Landmark Bonnie Parker's Old School, Lest the Remnants of Cement City Turn to Dust," *Dallas Morning News*, February 3, 2017; Popken, Amanda, "Eagle Ford School, Attended by the Infamous Bonnie Parker, is One Step Closer to Landmark Status," CandysDirt.com, February 7, 2017; interview, Joe Snowgold, caretaker of school.

Did Lone Star Lofts Serve as a SEAL Training Ground?
Jeppson, Noah, "Lon Star Gas Building Part I," *Unvisited Dallas*, July 16, 2010; Jeppson, Noah, "Lone Star Gas Building Part II," *Unvisited Dallas*, July 23, 2011; Mooney, Michael J, "Did SEAL Team Six Train in Dallas?" *D Magazine*, August 2013.

INDEX

1908 Trinity River flood, 49, 62, 84, 86, 144

1936 Centennial Texas State Fair, 142

508 Park Avenue, 30

880-yard race, 142

AARP, 14

AAU, 186–187

Afrika Korps, 12

All-American Boy, The, 76

Ambassador Hotel, 105, 168–169

America First Committee, 146

American Airlines Center, 34

Armstrong Commons, 76

Armstrong, Jack, 76

Armstrong, John, 44

Arts District, 10, 20, 44, 108, 114, 156, 168, 194

Arts Magnet School, 108

Asleep at the Wheel, 60

Atlantic Records, 6

Atmos Complex, 198

Autry, Gene "the Singing Cowboy", 114

Babb Brothers Barbeque, 68

Bachman Lake, 26

Badu, Erykah, 108, 166

Banks, Ernie, 108

Barlow, Clint, 166

Barrow, Clyde, 2, 20, 106–107

Barrow, Henry Basil, 106

Barrow, Marvin "Buck," 106

Baylor University Medical Center, 2

Be My Guest by Conrad Hilton, 170

Beatles, The, 19, 158–159

Belmont Motor Hotel, 54–55

Belo Garden, 152

Belo Mansion, 20

Belo, A. H., 20–21, 50

Benny, Jack, 64

Berry, Chuck, 82

Big Tex, 14–15, 70, 93, 116

Big Thicket Cabin, 12

Bin Laden, Osama, 198–199

Bishop Arts District, 44, 114, 168, 194

Black Dance Theater, 184

Blackstone Hotel, 64

Bob Wills and the Texas Playboys, 30

Bogart, Humphrey, 148

Bomb Factory, 166–167

Bond, James, 148

Booker T. Washington High School for the Performing and Visual Arts, 108–109, 112

Bowlski's, 160–161

Brandt, Gil, 178

Braniff Building, 66–67

Brass Knuckles Championship, 82

Brinker, Norman, 128

Bryan, John Neely, 126–127, 132

Burnett Field, 178–179

Busch, Adolphus, 64

business magnet school, 156

Cabana Motor Hotel, 158–159

Cabaniss, Edwin and Lisa, 114

Cadiz Street, 62, 80

Caesar's Palace, 158

Cagney, James, 148

Campisi, Joe, 4

Campisi, Carlo "Papa," 4

CANVAS Hotel, 84–85

carhops, 193
Carnegie Library, 50–51
Carnegie, Andrew, 50–51
Cartier watch, 122
Carver, George Washington, 16
Cash, Johnny, 82–83
caskets, 84
Cedars area, The, 154, 168
Centennial Celebration, 82
Centurion American, 159
Centurion American Development, 188
Chalk Hill Road, 196
Chapman, Ron, 18–19
Charles, Ray, 6–7
Chicks, The, 60
Chili's Restaurant, 128–129
Chitwood, Ida, 116
Civil War, 74, 84
Civilian Conservation Corps, 12
Clarence Saunders grocery stores, 44
Clarkson, Kelly, 60
Club Village, 42
Coca-Cola Bottling, 46
Cohn, Marc, 114
Cole, Nat King, 154
Cologix, 28
Color Kinetics, 46
Colored Knights of Pythias Temple, 16
Confederates, 74
Continental Bridge, 48–49
Continental Gin Building, 130–131
Coolidge, President Calvin, 147
Cooper Aerobics Center, 120–121
Cooper Institute, 120–121
Cooper, Dr. Kenneth, 120–121
Corey, "Professor" Irwin, 40

Cotton Machine Manufacturing Company, 130
Criswell, Dr. W. A., 10
Crozier Tech, 112, 156
Crystal Palace, 28
Cumberland Hill, 150–151
Curry, Bill, 82
D Magazine, 34, 61, 74, 128, 177
Dahl, George, 50
Dakota's Steakhouse, 10–11
Dallas Aloft Hotel, 162
Dallas Bar Association, 20–21
Dallas City Hall, 64–65
Dallas Coffin Company, 84–85
Dallas Colored High School, 108–109
Dallas County Administration Building, 22–23, 103
Dallas Cowboys, 5, 40, 178–179
Dallas Festival of the Arts, 38
Dallas Grand Hotel, 188
Dallas Heritage Village, 32–33, 159
Dallas High School, 112, 156–157
Dallas Morning News, The, 20, 50–51, 62, 87, 122, 178, 187
Dallas Running Club, 12
Dallas School Board, 150
Dallas Texans, 178
Dallas Theological Seminary, 2
Dallas Wonder, The, 186–187
Dallas World Aquarium, 90, 174–175
Dallas's City Federation of Women's Clubs, 50
Dallas's Employers Casualty Insurance Company (ECC), 186
Dallas's Farmers Market District, 80–81
DART, 56, 138–139, 156, 190
Davis Street, 114
Davis, Wirt, 46

David Crockett School, 24
Day, Doris, 158–159
de la Renta, Oscar, 74
Dealey Plaza, 22–23, 84, 132
Dedman Center, 76
DeGraw, Gavin, 160
Denison & Sherman Railway Company, 152
Dewey Groom and the Texas Longhorns, 114
DFW International Airport, 26, 67
Dick's Last Resort, 56
Didrikson, Babe, 186–187
Distinguished Service Cross, 118
Doak Walker Award, 76
Doak Walker Plaza, 76–77
Drakestone, 46–47
Dupont Plaza, 158
Eagle Ford Community, 196
Eat a Pig Sandwich, 192
Ebby's Place, 182–183
Egyptian Lounge, 4–5
Eiffel Tower, 122
El Centro College, 110–111
El Fenix Restaurants, 176–177
Encore Park, 30–31
Equinix, 28–29
Erasure, 160
Exposition Games, The, 142–143
Extall, Mrs. Henry, 50
Fair Park, 12, 14, 70–71, 112, 116, 184
Fair Park Fire Station, 72–73
Fairmont Hotel, 150
FBI, 106
Filter Building, 78–79
Firebird Restaurant Group, 176

Fisk Jubilee Singers, 16–17
Flexential, 28
Forest High School, 112
Four Seasons at the Las Colinas Sports Club, 164
Frogtown, 100, 140–141
Fuentes, Gloria and Jose, 192–193
Garcia del Moral, Javier, 194
Garland, Judy, 160
Garment Center, 162
Garvey, Marcus, 16
Gauguin, 134
German POW Camp, 12–13
Gloria's Restaurant, 192
Goat Hill, 122–123
Gobel, George, 40
Golden Cyclones basketball team, 186
Great Depression, The, 144, 192–193
Groom, Danny, 154
Guthrie, Arlo, 60
H. L. Green Variety Store, 172
Haggard, Merle, 154
Hagman, Larry, 132
Halliday, Ebby, 182
Hamilton Properties, 46, 198–199
Hardwell, 166
Harry Hines, 66–67, 124–125
Hart, Gary, 82
Hartgraves, Mrs. Alcie, 2
Hartgraves Café, 2–3
Harvest, The, 80
Hefner, Christie, 40
Heisman Trophy, 76
"Hellhound on My Trail," 30
Hendrix, Jimi, 158–159
Heymann, Claire, 74–75

Hill, Lauryn, 166

Hilton, Conrad, 170–171

Hispanic Association of Colleges and Universities, 110

Hoblitzelle Foundation, 148

Hoffa, Jimmy, 158–159

Hogan, Ben, 164

Holiday Inn, 170

Hope, Bob, 64, 148

Hotel Indigo, 170–171

Hotel St. Germain, 74–75

Houdini, Harry, 148

House of Blues, 136–137

Houston Street Viaduct, 62–63, 144

Hyatt House Hotel, The, 158

Indio Management, 24

Ingram Freezer Building, 162

Inn of the Dove, The, 184–185

Interstate Theatre Company, 148

Interurban Railway, 44–45, 138, 152–153

Interurban Train Station, 88, 152–153

Italian Village, 42

J. Erik Jonsson Central Library, 152

Jackson, Dr. Reuben, 192

Jackson, Michael, 188

Jaffe, Sarah, 166

James, Frank, 110

James, Jesse, 58–59

James Madison High School, 112–113

Jefferson Boulevard, 44–45, 50–53, 178–179

Jefferson St. Viaduct, 48, 53

Jefferson, Henry Lemon "Blind Lemon," 6, 17

JFK Memorial, 132

John Dick Aviation Concentration Camp, 70–71

John Sexton and Company, 22

Johnson, Robert, 30

Jolson, Al, 86

Joker, notification system, 72

Kazan, Lainie, 40

Keith and Margo's Murder Mystery, 116

Kennedy assassination, 1, 4, 22, 52, 124, 154

Kessler Theater, 114–115

Kessler, George, 144

Kidd Springs Fishing and Boating Club, 38–39

Kidd, "Colonel" James, 38

Kidz Bop, 136

Kim Dawson Studios, 28

King's Village, 42

Kingston, Texas, 118

Kirby, Jesse, 192

KLIF, the "Mighty 1190," 1, 18–19, 45

Klyde Warren Park, 34, 48

Kompan Blox playground, 48

L.A. Times, 4

L.A. Olympic Games, 187

La Tunisia Restaurant, 66

LaFrance, Jay, 154

Lake Cliff Park, 86–87, 99

Lake, Jim, 168

Lakewood Country Club, 164–165

Lakewood Theater, 160–161

Lamar-McKinney Viaduct, 48–49

Lauper, Cyndi, 160

Law, Don, 30

Ledbetter, Huddie William "Lead Belly," 6

Led Zeppelin, 158–159

Liberty Radio Network, 18

Light Crust Doughboys, The, 30

Lincoln Properties, 10

Lindbergh Drive, 146–147

Lipscomb Elementary School, 146

Little Egypt, 36–37

Little Egypt Baptist Church, 36

Little Mexico, 34, 150, 176

Live and Let Die, 148

Lolo Cavazos, 30

Lone Star Gas Lofts, 198–199

Long, Wooden Bridge, The, 62–63

Longhorn Ballroom, The, 154–155

Loudermilk-Sparkman Funeral Home, 20

Love Field, 26–27, 66, 70, 146–147, 182

Love, 2LT Moss Lee, 26

Lucky Lindy, 146

LULAC National Educational Services, Inc, 180–181

Lynn, Loretta, 154–155

Magnolia Petroleum Building, 8–9, 47

Majestic Theatre, 148–149

Malcolm X Boulevard, 6

Mallory Drug Store, 44–45

Mangold, Charles, 86

Marcus, Herbert, 110, 134

Marcus, Stanley, 112, 134

Margaret Hunt Hill Bridge, 48, 68–69

Market Hall, 28

Marsalis, Thomas, 44

Martin Luther King Jr. Blvd., 112

Martinez, Alfred, 176

Martinez, Mike, 176

Matthews Southwest, 156–157

Max Orlopp of Orlopp & Kusener Architecture, 132

Mayhew Machine and Engineering Works, 166–167

Mays, Willie, 178

McCombs, Col. M. J., 186

McCutcheon, Attorney General Currie, 140

McLachlan, Sarah, 24

McLendon, Gordon, 18

McShain, Danny, 82

Melcher, Martin, 158

Mexican American Historical League, 196

Mickey Mantle's Bowling Center, 66

Midway Road, 118–119

Miller, William Brown, 32

Millermore Mansion, The, 32–33

Mineola, Texas, 160

Moayedi, Mehrdad, 159

Mockingbird Lane, 4–5, 146–147

Monroe Shops, 138–139

Moody, Dan, 146–147

Morrison, Helen Belo, 20

Munger, Robert, 130–131

Murphy, 1LT Audie, 118–119

Murphy, John Patrick, 74

Murrow, Edward R., 134

N. R. Crozier Technical High School, 156

Naval Special Warfare Development Group, 198

Negro Motorist Green Book, The, 184–185

Neiman Marcus, 47, 110, 134–135

Nelms, O. L., 154–155

Nelson, Byron, 164–165

New Deal, 12

Newman, David "Fathead," 6

Nichols Mansion, 121

Nightcaps, The, 160

Northlake Shopping Center, 36–37

Northpark Mall, 134–135

NYLO Hotel, 84–85

O'Brien, Jim, 18

Oak Cliff, 36, 38, 44–46, 48, 50–53, 62–63, 86, 114, 144–145, 168, 180, 186–187, 193

Oak Cliff Chamber of Commerce, The, 114

213

Oak Cliff Country Club, 164
Oak Cliff Methodist Church, 44
Oak Cliff Viaduct, 62
Oak Lawn Village, 42
Old City Park, 32–33
Old Dallas Public Library, 50
Old Mill Restaurant, 116–117
Old Red Courthouse, 132–133, 145
Old Scotchman, The, 18
Old Tige, 72–73
Omni Hotel, 8
Opera House, 122
Oswald, Lee Harvey, 1, 4, 23, 52, 124, 132, 154
Pachanga Wholesale Bridal and Quinceañera, 44–45, 92
Pan-Am Games, 142–143
Paris, 18, 74, 122, 172
Park Plaza, 188
Parker, Bonnie, 2, 106, 197
Parkland Memorial Hospital, 124–125
Payne, Darwin, 6
PC Cobb Stadium, 28–29
Pearl Beer, 122
Pearl Harbor, 146
Pegasus Plaza, 8
Perot Museum, 34, 140
Petta, Victor Jr., 56
PGA, 164
Pickford, Mary, 148
Pig Stand Restaurant, 192–193
Pittman, The, 16–17
Pittman, William Sydney, 16–17
Plant, Robert, 166
Playboy Club, 40–41
Ponca City, Oklahoma, 58
Prather, Coy, 154

Premier Boxing Champions Super Welterweight World Championship, 167
Presidential Scholars, 108
Presley, Elvis, 82
Preston Center, 134–135
Preston Trail, 164
Price Is Right, The, 18
Prince Albert of Monaco, 74
Principal Residences, 24–25
Purity Journal, The, 140
Queen Anne, 74
Queen Elizabeth II, 64
Queen of the Bandits, 58
Ramones, 166
Red Hot Chili Peppers, The, 154
Reed, Jim, 58–59
Republic Bank, 20, 46, 190
Republic Bank Building, 46–47
Republic Center, 191
Revival Tabernacle, 114
Robinson, Elroy, 142
"rocket, the," 190–191
Rocky Horror Picture Show, The, 160
Roddy, Rod, 18
Rodgers, Woodall, 140–141
Romanesque Revival, 22
Rommel, General Erwin, 12
Ronald Kirk Bridge, 48–49
Rooney, Mickey, 160
Roosevelt, President Franklin, 12
Ruby, Jack, 4–5, 124, 154
Saint Ann Restaurant, 34–35
Saint Ann's School, 34–35
Sanger Brothers Building, The, 110
Santa Fe Building, 94, 162
Scyene Road, 58–59

SEAL Team Six, 198

Sears, 84

SEDCO Oil Company, 150

Sedimentation Basins, 78–79

Sex Pistols, 154

Shacktown, 126

Shed, The, 80

Sheen, Martin, 46

Shirley, John and Elizabeth, 58

Shoemaker, David, *Squared Circle: Life, Death, and Professional Wrestling*, 82

Simpson, Sturgill, 166

Sinatra, Frank, 6, 188

Singleton Blvd., 68, 107

Sixth Floor Museum, 22–23, 132

Skillman, W. F., 146

SMU, 41, 63, 65, 76–77, 142, 145, 165

SMU East Campus, 40–41

Sons of Hermann Hall, 60–61

Southern Rock Island Plow Company, 22

Southland Corporation, 128, 181

Southwest's Greatest Playground, The, 86–87

Spaghetti Warehouse, The, 56–57

Spanish Flu, 70

speakeasy, 168

Spelling, Aaron, 112

Spivey, Craig and Jennifer, 160

Sportatorium, 82–83

Spirit of St. Louis, 146–147

St. Louis, 64, 144

Stallworth, Dave, 112

Stanfield, Sylvia, 112

Star Service Station, 106

Starr, Belle, 58–59

State Fair of Texas, 14, 71

Statler Hilton and Residences, 188–189

Statler Hilton, The, 159, 188–189

Statue of Liberty, 122

Stemmons Frwy., 29, 122–123, 158–159

Stemmons, Leslie, 145

Stephen F. Austin, 56

Stewart, Martha, 74

Strickland Transportation Company, 68

Sturges, Preston, 70–71

Styx, 188

Sunset High School, 44

Sylvan Thirty Apartments, 54

Taylor Lofts, 80

Texas Baseball League, 46

Texas Centennial Exposition, The, 116

Texas School Book Depository, 22–23, 122

Texas Theatre, 22, 52–53, 114

Texas Victory Open, 164–165

Texas's first high school football team, 109

Thompson, Joe C. "Jodie," 180

Thornton, R. L., 14

Time Magazine, 147

Titche-Goettinger Company, 172

Tootsie, 104, 134–135

Tormé, Mel, 40

Tote'm Store, 180

Tracy-Locke, 122, 180

Trailways Bus Company, 152

Traveling Riverside Blues, 30

Travis Elementary, 150

Trees Dallas, 166

Triangle Building, 18

Trinity Cement Company, 196

Trinity Forest Golf Club, 164

Trinity Groves, 68–69, 145

Trinity Levee District, 144

Trinity River, 44, 46, 48–49, 62–63, 68, 126, 140, 144–145, 178

Trinity River Project, 48

Ulrickson Committee, 144–145

UT Southwestern Medical School, 67

Vacuum Oil Company, 8

Vaudeville, 148–149

Ventura, Sam, 42–43

Victory Fair, 71

Victory Park, 136

Victory Plaza, 158

Village Club, 42

Vique, Paco, 194

Von Erich, David, 82

Von Erich, Fritz, 82

Von Erich, Kerry, 82

Von Erich, Kevin, 82

W. A. Green Department Store, 172

Walker, Doak, 76–77

Warner Brothers, 148

West Dallas, 48–49, 54, 68, 106–107

West End, 56, 132, 140–141, 174

White Rock Boathouse Facility, 78

White Rock Creek, 78

White Rock Lake, 1, 12, 36, 78–79, 146–147, 164

White Swan Coffee Processing, 136–137

White, Dwight, 112

Wild Detectives Bookstore, 194–195

Wills, Bob, 30, 154–155

Wilson Building, 172–173

Winfrey Point, 12–13

WiNGS (Women in Need of Generous Support), 182–183

Woodall Rogers Freeway, 48, 150, 174, 176

Woodrow Wilson High School, 160

Woodruff, John, 142

World Championship Chili Cook-Off at Terlingua, Texas, 128

World War II, 12, 42, 112, 118, 132, 146, 151, 166, 180, 184, 194–195

World's Fair, 28

WPA, 28

Wright Model C Pusher biplane, 26